Y0-DNR-117

Feeding the Flock

2015

A Collection of Recipes by
First Missionary Baptist Church
1421 Wilson Ave.
Oildale, CA 93308

Printed in the USA by

MORRIS PRESS
COOKBOOKS

800-445-6621 • www.morriscookbooks.com
P.O. Box 2110 • Kearney, NE 68848

126207-tb   1

In Appreciations

There is no way we can thank all of our wonderful Women's Fellowship ladies for their participation in this book. The Lord had blessed us so much. We want this book to show our love and dedication to His work. We hope this book gives a few chuckles and some real blessing to those who buy it.

There is a special bond among those who break bread together, a custom established by our Lord Jesus Christ. We hope this collection of recipes will bless those who use them.

Recipe From Pastor Ken

My recipe is for **"The Best of Life."** Begin by adding one "new heart." Blend in God's word. Stir frequently with prayer. Pour a full cup of the Holy Spirit, two cups if you like a smoother texture. Add a large measure of God's love and a handful of grace. Allow to rise gently, and serve yourself, your family, and your world a slice of the best of life! I've tried it, and its joy is unspeakable and full of glory.

Peace be with you,
Pastor Ken

Table Blessings

Table Grace
We thank you God for happy hearts,
For rain and sunny weather.
We thank you God for this, our food,
And that we are together.

Grace
(to the tune of Edelweiss)
Bless our friends, bless our food,
Come, O Lord, and sit with us.

May our speech, glow with peace,
And your love surround us.

Bless our friends, bless our food,
Come, O Lord, and be with us.

Heaven's Grocery Store

I was walking down life's highway a long time ago,
One day I saw a sign that read "Heaven's Grocery Store."
As I got a little closer, the door came open wide.
And when I came to myself, I was standing there inside.

I saw a host of angels, they were standing everywhere,
One handed me a basket and said, "My child, shop with care."
Everything a Christian needed was in that grocery store,
And all you couldn't carry, you could come back for more.

First, I got some patience, love was in the same row,
Further down was understanding, you need that wherever you go.
I got a box or two of wisdom and a bag or two of faith,
I just couldn't miss the Holy Ghost, for it was all over the place.

I stopped to get some strength and courage, to help me run
    the race.
By then my basket was getting full, but I remembered I needed
    some grace.
I didn't forget salvation, for salvation, that was free,
So I tried to get enough of that to save both you and me.
Then I started up to the counter to pay my grocery bill,
For I thought I had everything to do my Master's will.

As I went up the aisle, I saw prayer and just had to put that in,
For I knew when I stepped outside, I would run right into sin.
Peace and joy were all plentiful, they were on the last shelf,
Song and praises were hanging near, so I just helped myself.

Then I said to the angel, "Now how much do I owe?"
He just smiled and said, "Just take them everywhere you go."
Again, I smiled at him and said, "How much do I owe?"
He smiled again and said, "My child, Jesus paid your bill a long
    time ago."

A Recipe for the Good Life

A heaping cup of Kindness
    Two cups of Love and Caring
    One cup of Understanding
    One cup of Joyful Sharing

A level cup of Patience
    One cup of Thoughtful Insight
    One cup of Gracious Listening
    One cup of Sweet Forgiveness

Mix ingredients together
    Toss in Smiles and Laughter
    Serve to everyone you know
    with Love forever after.

Table of Contents

Appetizers
& Beverages

Helpful Hints

- Add flavor to tea by dissolving old-fashioned lemon drops or hard mint candies in it. They melt quickly and keep the tea brisk.

- Make your own spiced tea or cider. Place orange peels, whole cloves, and cinnamon sticks in a 6-inch square piece of cheesecloth. Gather the corners and tie with a string. Steep in hot cider or tea for 10 minutes; steep longer if you want a stronger flavor.

- Always chill juices or sodas before adding them to beverage recipes.

- Calorie-free club soda adds sparkle to iced fruit juices and reduces calories per portion.

- To cool your punch, float an ice ring made from the punch rather than using ice cubes. It appears more decorative, prevents diluting, and does not melt as quickly.

- Place fresh or dried mint in the bottom of a cup of hot chocolate for a cool and refreshing taste.

- When making fresh lemonade or orange juice, one lemon yields about ¼ cup juice, while one orange yields about ⅓ cup juice.

- Never boil coffee; it brings out acids and causes a bitter taste. Store ground coffee in the refrigerator or freezer to keep it fresh.

- Always use cold water for electric drip coffee makers. Use 1–2 tablespoons ground coffee for each cup of water.

- How many appetizers should you prepare? Allow 4–6 appetizers per guest if a meal quickly follows. If a late meal is planned, allow 6–8 appetizers per guest. If no meal follows, allow 8–10 pieces per guest.

- If serving appetizers buffet-style or seating is limited, consider no-mess finger foods that don't require utensils to eat.

- Think "outside the bowl." Choose brightly-colored bowls to set off dips or get creative with hollowed-out loaves of bread, bell peppers, heads of cabbage, or winter squash.

- Cheeses should be served at room temperature – approximately 70°.

- To keep appetizers hot, make sure you have enough oven space and warming plates to maintain their temperature.

- To keep appetizers cold, set bowls on top of ice or rotate bowls of dips from the fridge every hour or as needed.

APPETIZERS & BEVERAGES

CREAMY TARRAGON DIP

1 (8-oz.) pkg. cream cheese,
  softened
½ c. mayonnaise
¼ c. milk
4 tsp. tarragon vinegar
1 tsp. sugar
¾ tsp. salt

⅛ tsp. pepper
Carrot sticks
Chinese pea pods
Romaine lettuce leaves
Cauliflowerets
Zucchini slices

In a blender at low speed or in food process or knife blade attached, blend first 8 ingredients until smooth. Pour mixture into small bowl. Cover and refrigerate. To serve, line a large basket with a deep dish or foil. Arrange vegetables and bowl of dip in basket. If dip becomes too thick upon refrigeration, stir in a little milk until it reaches dipping consistency. Serves 10. Yield: about 2 cups. Start about 1 hour before serving or early in day.

LAYERED TACO DIP
Glenda Harwell

1 can bean dip
1 recipe guacamole dip
1 lb. sour cream
1 c. Cheddar cheese, shredded
1 pkg. taco seasoning

1 c. shredded Jack cheese
1 c. chopped tomatoes
¼ c. green onions
1 can chopped olives

Guacamole Dip: Mash 2 avocados. Add 1 teaspoon lemon juice, ¼ cup salsa and a dash of salt. Mix until creamy. **Layered Dip:** Add taco seasoning to the sour cream; mix well and set aside. Spread the bean dip evenly on a plate or platter. Add the guacamole to the top of the bean dip and spread smoothly. Next spread the sour cream and taco seasoning mixture to the top of the guacamole. Sprinkle the Cheddar cheese on top of the sour cream. Add the chopped tomatoes. Layer the olives.

CHEESE BALL
Lucy Bowen

2 (8-oz.) pkgs. cream cheese
½ lb. sharp Cheddar cheese
1 handful green onions, chopped
2 tsp. pimiento
1 tsp. spicy brown mustard

1 tsp. lemon juice
2 tsp. Worcestershire sauce
Paprika
1 sm. can deviled ham or chicken
Walnuts

Mix all together and roll into a ball. Chill. Roll in walnuts.

LAYERED BEAN DIP

1 (16-oz.) can fat-free refried beans
1 (15-oz.) can black beans, rinsed
  and drained
½ c. reduced fat sour cream

1 c. bottled salsa
1 c. (4 oz.) pre-shredded blend or
  cheddar cheese
Chopped cilantro (opt.)

(continued)

Preheat oven to 375°. Combine beans; spread in an 8-inch baking dish. Spread sour cream over beans. Top with salsa and add cheese. Cover; bake at 375° for 20 minutes. Uncover; bake 10 minutes, or until bubbly. Garnish with cilantro if desired. **Tip:** To make pita chips, cut 5 (6-inch) onion-flavored or regular pitas into 8 wedges each. Arrange on a baking sheet coated with cooking spray. Lightly coat tops of wedges with cooking spray. Sprinkle with ½ teaspoon garlic powder and ¼ teaspoon salt. Bake at 375° for 8 minutes, or until lightly browned. Yield: about 2 ½ cups dip, serving size ¼ cup.

SPICY CHICKEN WINGS

24 chicken wings	**1 tsp. catsup**
⅓ c. butter or margarine, melted	**½ tsp. garlic powder**
3 T. Tabasco sauce	**Blue cheese dip**

Remove and discard tips from chicken wings. Cut wings apart at joint to make 48 pieces. Place chicken pieces on wire racks over drip pans. Pre-bake in preheated 350° oven for 1 ½ hours, turning after 45 minutes. Meanwhile, combine butter, Tabasco, catsup and garlic powder; mix well. When wings are done, toss pieces in butter mixture; serve hot or at room temperature with blue cheese dip. Serves 6.

FRIED CATFISH APPETIZERS

1 ½ lbs. catfish fillets	**⅔ c. yellow cornmeal**
⅔ c. lemon juice	**2 tsp. salt**
2 tsp. Tabasco sauce	**Oil for deep frying**
⅔ c. all-purpose flour	**Hot pepper sauce**

Cut fillets crosswise into ¾-inch strips. Blend lemon juice and Tabasco in shallow dish; add fish and marinate 45 minutes. Combine flour, cornmeal and salt. Coat drained fish with mixture. In large skillet, heat oil 1 ½ inches deep to 350°. Deep-fry fish until golden brown on all sides; drain well on paper towels. Serve with hot pepper sauce if desired. **Tip:** Haddock or halibut may be substituted if catfish is not available. Serves 6 to 8.

PEACH-GLAZED MEATBALLS

2 eggs, lightly beaten	**1 ½ lbs. ground beef**
1 (8-oz.) can water chestnuts,	**1 (16-oz.) jar peach preserves**
drained and chopped	**1 (12-oz.) bottle chili sauce**
¾ c. dry bread crumbs	**1 env. onion soup mix**
1 T. beef bouillon granules	

In a large bowl, combine the eggs, water chestnuts, bread crumbs and bouillon. Crumble beef over mixture and mix well. Shape into 1-inch balls. In a large skillet, cook meatballs in batches until no longer pink; drain. Return all to the skillet. In a small saucepan, combine the preserves, chili sauce and soup mix. Cook over medium-low heat for 5 minutes. Pour over meatballs. Simmer, uncovered, for 10 minutes, or until heated through. Makes about 4 ½ dozen.

126207-15

PIZZA ENGLISH MUFFINS

1 lb. ground beef
¾ lb. bulk pork sausage
1 sm. onion, chopped
½ c. tomato paste
½ tsp. garlic salt
½ tsp. dried oregano
¼ tsp. cayenne pepper

3 (12-oz.) pkgs. English muffins,
  split
1 ½ c. (6 oz.) shredded part-skim
  mozzarella cheese
1 c. (4 oz.) shredded cheddar
  cheese
1 c. (4 oz.) shredded Swiss cheese

Cook ground beef, sausage and onion over medium heat until meat is no longer pink; drain. Stir in the tomato paste, garlic salt, oregano and cayenne. Spread over the cut side of each cayenne. Spread over the cut side of each English muffin. Place on baking sheets. Combine the cheeses; sprinkle over meat mixture. Freeze for up to 3 months or bake at 350° for 15 to 20 minutes, or until heated through. To use frozen English Muffins, bake at 350° for 30 minutes. Makes 3 dozen. Preparation time: 35 minutes.

BACON CHEESEBURGER BUNS

2 (¼-oz.) pkgs. active dry yeast
⅔ c. warm water (110° to 115°)
⅔ c. warm milk (110° to 115°)
¼ c. sugar

¼ c. shortening
2 eggs
2 tsp. salt
4 ½ to 5 c. all-purpose flour

Filling:

1 lb. sliced bacon, diced
2 lbs. ground beef
1 sm. onion, chopped
2 lbs. ground beef
1 sm. onion, chopped
1 ½ tsp. salt

½ tsp. pepper
1 lb. process cheese (Velveeta),
  cubed
3 to 4 T. butter, melted
Ketchup or barbecue sauce (opt.)

In a large bowl, dissolve yeast in warm water. Add the milk, sugar, shortening, eggs, salt and 3 ½ cups flour; beat until smooth. Stir in enough remaining flour to form a soft dough. Turn onto a floured surface; knead until smooth and elastic, 6 to 8 minutes. Place in a greased bowl, turning once to grease top. Cover and let rise in a warm place until doubled, about 1 hour. Meanwhile, in a large skillet, cook bacon over medium heat until crisp. Using a slotted spoon, remove to paper towels. In a Dutch oven, cook the beef, onion, salt and pepper over medium heat until meat is no longer pink; drain. Add bacon and cheese. Cook and stir until cheese is melted. Remove from the heat. Punch dough down. Turn onto a lightly floured surface; divide in fourths. Roll each portion into a 12 x 8-inch rectangle. Cut each into 6 squares. Place ¼ cup meat mixture in the center of each square. Bring corners together in the center and pinch to seal. Place 2 inches apart on greased baking sheets. Bake at 400° for 9 to 11 minutes, or until lightly browned. Brush with butter. Serve warm with ketchup if desired. Makes 2 dozen. Preparation time: 1 hour plus rising.

FRUITY-LIMEADE SLUSH
(Diabetic)

Lucy Bowen

1 lime
3 c. water
4 (2.2g) pkts. low calorie cherry-
  limeade mix

3 c. ice
2 c. frozen mixed berries
4 lime wedges

Finely shred 1 teaspoon peel from the whole lime. Squeeze juice from lime into blender. Add peel, water and dry drink mix. Cover and blend until mix is dissolved. Add ice and mixed berries. Cover and blend until mixture and ice is crushed. Pour into glasses and garnish with lime wedges.

MAY ROBISON'S PARTY PUNCH

1 gal. Hi-C or Hawaiian Punch
2 L. 7-Up

½ gal. sherbet

Mix punch and 7-Up together, then float sherbet on top. Depending on your color theme: Green punch, lime sherbet; orange punch, orange sherbet; pink/red punch, raspberry sherbet; any color punch, rainbow sherbet.

MAY ROBISON'S LEMONADE

6 ½ c. water
1 c. lemon juice
1 c. sugar

4 scoops Country Time
1 lemon, peeled and cut into sm.
  pieces

Refrigerate or serve over ice. Makes 2 quarts.

DIP FOR APPLES

Sandra Kester

2 pkgs. cream cheese
1 tsp. vanilla

4 T. brown sugar

Mix all together with mixer for 2 minutes, or until all is blended well. Serve sliced apples (green or red). Delicious. They will come back for more.

CRISPIX "PARTY" MIX ORIGINAL RECIPE

Rhonda Pierce

7 c. Crispix cereal
1 c. pretzels
¼ tsp. garlic salt
2 tsp. lemon juice

1 c. mixed nuts
3 T. margarine, melted
¼ tsp. onion salt
4 tsp. Worcestershire sauce

Combine Crispix cereal, nuts and pretzels in a 13 x 9 x 2-inch baking pan and set aside. Stir together remaining ingredients. Gently stir spices and margarine into cereal mixture until evenly coated. Bake at 250° for about 45 minutes, stirring every 15 minutes. Spread on paper towels to cool. Store in airtight container. Makes 9 cups and serves 10 to 12 people. **Tip:** Dry roasted mixed nuts may be used in place of regular mixed nuts and reduced calorie margarine for regular margarine. Can also use Chex cereal instead of Crispix cereal.

126207-15

GOLDEN GRAHAM SNACK

4 c. Golden Grahams
1 ½ c. miniature marshmallows
1 c. (16 oz.) semisweet chips

⅓ c. light corn syrup
1 T. butter
½ tsp. vanilla extract

In a large bowl, combine cereal and marshmallows; set aside. Place the chocolate chips, corn syrup and butter in a 1-quart microwavable dish. Microwave, uncovered, on high for 1 to 2 minutes, or until smooth, stirring every 30 seconds. Stir in the vanilla. Pour over cereal mixture and mix well. Drop by tablespoonfuls onto waxed paper-lined baking sheets. Cool.

PEACH OR BERRY SMOOTHIES   *Lucy Bowen*

2 c. fresh sliced peaches, nectarines
   or apricots
1 (6-oz.) ctn. fat-free yogurt

1 c. sm. ice cubes or crushed ice
1 c. fat-free milk

In a blender, combine fruit, milk and yogurt until mixture is smooth. Gradually add ice, blending until smooth and thick.

CHEESE SAUCE   *Betty Montgomery*

1 c. milk
2 T. butter

2 T. flour
1 c. grated Velveeta cheese

Heat milk 2 minutes on medium; set aside. Melt butter on high and stir in flour. Stir 1 more minute on high. Stir in warm milk and blend well. Cook 2½ minutes, until boils. Turn off fire. Stir in cheese and blend.

DEVILED EGGS   *Rhonda Pierce*
(Mayonnaise)

12 hard-boiled eggs
½ tsp. pepper
2 T. dill pickle juice
1 can black olives, slicing 6 olives
   in half (opt.)

½ tsp. salt
2 T. mustard
⅓ c. mayonnaise

Boil 12 eggs. Crack and peel shell, then rinse eggs off to make sure no shell is left on them. Cut the eggs in half and take out center yolks and put in a bowl. After all yolks are in bowl, add salt and pepper, then mash yolks to a dry mix consistency. Add mayonnaise, mustard and pickle juice, mixing together thoroughly. Taste to see if you need to add any more mayonnaise or mustard. Be careful not to overdo it. Put in candy/icing decorator (or plastic bag cutting a corner off). Place egg yolks on plate with small bowl of olives in middle of plate. Fill egg halves with egg mixture on plate, then place a olive half on top of each deviled egg. When completed, put in refrigerator until ready to serve.

CHILI CON CUSO

Kelly Edwards

1 lb. Velveeta cheese
4 cloves garlic or ½ tsp. garlic
   powder

1 lg. onion
1 sm. can diced Ortega chilies
1 (16-oz.) can stewed tomatoes

Dice onions and sauté in a tablespoon of shortening or vegetable oil. After onions are transparent, add garlic and simmer until garlic is cooked. Then put Ortega chilies and tomatoes in a strainer and squeeze between your fingers until the juice is drained. Then add the mixture to the onions. Add Velveeta cheese until completely melted. Serve in fondue dish with tortilla chips.

STUFFED JALAPEÑO PEPPERS

Kelly Edwards

1 can marinated jalapeños
1 can white tuna

½ c. mayonnaise

Drain can of jalapeños and cut in half lengthwise. Mix tuna and mayonnaise together and fill jalapeños. Chill and enjoy.

BLACK BEAN DIP

Kelly Edwards

1 can Progresso cooked black
   beans, rinsed and drained
½ c. favorite picante sauce or salsa

¼ pkg. Lawry's burrito seasoning
   mix

Add ingredients to a little food processor and blend until smooth. Put in microwavable dish; heat through and serve with tortilla chips topped with melted cheese.

SALSA MADE EASY

Kelly Edwards

2 cans Mexican stewed tomatoes
2 T. hot diced jalapeños
1 med. diced yellow onion

Generous amount of salt and
   pepper
Pinch of sugar

Cut up the onion. Place all ingredients in blender and blend. Add more jalapeños if you want a little spice in your life!! Serve with chips and guacamole. We like it in soup, too.

CHILI CHEESE DIP

Kelly Edwards

1 can Hormel no-bean chili
8 oz. cream cheese
¾ c. shredded Jack cheese

2 green onions (opt.)
1 sm. can sliced olives (opt.)
½ can diced chilies (opt.)

Mix chili with chunked up cream cheese. Heat in microwave until blended, approximately 2 minutes. Top with shredded cheese, onions and Ortega chilies. You can use any combination of the last 3 ingredients. Serve warm with your favorite tortilla chips.

6

BLT PIZZA

Kelly Edwards

1 pkg. traditional pizza dough
(Pillsbury ready-made)
8 slices bacon, cooked crisp
4 tomatoes, chopped coarse

½ sm. chopped head iceberg lettuce
4 to 6 T. mayonnaise
Salt and pepper to taste

Preheat oven to 425°. Place dough on baking sheet. Cut bacon into pieces. Mix bacon, lettuce and tomato and season to taste. Spread mixture over dough. Bake 20 minutes. Garnish with additional lettuce if desired. Serve at once.

DALLAS COWBOY GUACAMOLE

Kelly Edwards

3 ripe avocados, peeled and seeded
2 fresh green chilies, stemmed,
seeded and chopped, or 1
jalapeño

1 clove garlic, chopped fine
10 sprigs cilantro, chopped
½ tsp. salt
½ lime, juiced

Mash avocados. Add remaining ingredients and mix well. Serve with favorite tortilla chips.

HENNESSEE'S SALSA

Kelly Edwards

1 (22-oz.) can whole tomatoes
3 jalapeño peppers
½ bunch of cilantro

3 to 4 green onions
2 cloves garlic
Salt to taste

Boil jalapeños for 7 to 8 minutes. Remove stems (don't touch peppers directly with your hands). Place peppers in a blender with tomatoes, can garlic. Liquefy. Remove and add to a bowl. Cut up fresh cilantro and green onions. Cilantro bunches vary in size. I use about ½ bunch to the entire bunch. When time permits, I rub peppers and garlic with olive oil and roast in pie pan in the oven at 400° for 20 minutes, or until they look and smell right. Garnish with sprig of cilantro and serve with tortilla chips.

7-LAYER TEX MEX DIP

Kelly Edwards

2 cans spicy bean dip
1 pt. sour cream
1 pkg. taco seasoning
3 to 4 avocados
1 tsp. mayonnaise
Lemon juice

2 to 3 T. salsa
2 c. grated Cheddar cheese
3 diced tomatoes
4 to 5 scallions
1 sm. can diced olives

Spread beans on bottom of 9 x 13-inch pan. Mix sour cream and package of taco seasoning. Spread over beans. Mix avocado, mayonnaise, lemon juice and salsa. Spread over sour cream. Sprinkle cheese over the top. Layer with the remaining ingredients; tomatoes, scallions and olives. Serve with your favorite tortilla chips.

POCKET PIZZA

Kelly Edwards

Pizza Dough:

1 c. flour
⅓ c. milk
2 T. oil

1 tsp. baking powder
½ tsp. salt

Beat all ingredients in a bowl until the dough pulls away from the side of the bowl. Turn onto a lightly floured surface; gather into a ball. Knead 10 times. Cover with a bowl and let stand 15 minutes.

Topping:

1 T. vegetable oil
¼ c. pizza sauce
1 c. shredded mozzarella cheese
½ c. cooked Italian sausage

1 T. finely chopped onion
⅛ to ¼ tsp. garlic powder
¼ pkg. (3 oz.) sliced pepperoni
2 to 3 T. pizza sauce

Heat the oven to 425°. Lightly grease a cookie sheet with shortening. Prepare pizza dough. Roll into a 12-inch circle. Fold loosely in half. Place on cookie sheet and unfold; brush with oil. Layer remaining ingredients on half the circle in order listed. Fold dough over filling. Turn edge at the lower dough over edge of the top dough. Pinch edge to seal. Prick top with fork. Bake until golden brown, 20 to 25 minutes.

SHRIMP COCKTAIL

Alice B.

1 c. celery, chopped very fine
½ c. onion, dehydrated
3 T. Worcestershire sauce
5 T. lemon juice
1 bottle cocktail sauce

½ bottle catsup (1 to 1½ c.)
Shrimp or crab, drained if canned (I use sm. pre-cooked from heat counter, about 1 or 2 lbs.)

Mix all ingredients together. Serve cold.

WASSAIL

Alice Banning

2 qt. warm water
2 scant c. sugar, dissolve in water
12 oz. frozen orange juice
½ c. lemon juice

2 sticks cinnamon
1 button ginger
10 allspice beans

Boil spices in 1 quart water, then strain.

1½ gal. apple cider

Warm all together. Makes 20 small cups. Keep and use water from spices and toss spices away.

8

SHRIMP COCKTAIL SAUCE

Alice Banning

1 c. celery, chopped fine
½ c. onion
3 T. Worcestershire sauce
5 T. lemon juice

1 bottle cocktail sauce
½ bottle catsup (1 to 1 ½ c.)
Shrimp or crab or both

Mix all ingredients. Add cooked shrimp. Stir together. Serve chilled. No cooking.

SWEET & SOUR MEATBALLS

Alice Banning

Mix and stir thoroughly in deep sauce pot:

1 can whole cranberry sauce

1 bottle chili sauce

Heat to boiling point.

Mix:

2 lbs. ground beef
2 eggs
Salt and pepper
1 med. fine chopped onion

Cornflakes, crumbled, enough to
hold together meatballs, about 1
c.

Shape into small meatballs and drop into hot sauce, one at a time. Do not stir. Simmer about 1 hour. Sauce will bubble over the meatballs. After they have begun cooking, stir very little and gently. They have a tendency to break apart if stirred too soon.

LEMON-GARLIC BROILED SHRIMP

2 lbs. shrimp, shelled and deveined
2 cloves garlic, minced
½ c. butter or margarine
3 T. lemon juice

½ tsp. salt
Pinch of black pepper
Chopped parsley

Rinse shrimp well with cold water; drain. Sauté onion in butter until tender; remove from heat and stir in lemon juice, salt and pepper. Arrange shrimp in single layer in large shallow baking pan; pour sauce over shrimp. Broil 4 inches from heat 8 to 10 minutes, or until shrimp are pink and tender. Baste once with sauce in pan. Sprinkle with parsley and serve as appetizer or main course. Serves 6.

Recipe Favorites

126207-15

Soups & Salads

Helpful Hints

- If the soup is not intended as the main course, count on 1 quart to serve 6. As the main dish, plan on 1 quart to serve 2.

- After cooking vegetables, pour any water and leftover vegetable pieces into a freezer container. When full, add tomato juice and seasoning to create a money-saving "free soup."

- Instant potatoes help thicken soups and stews.

- A leaf of lettuce dropped in a pot of soup absorbs grease from the top – remove the lettuce and serve. You can also make soup the day before, chill, and scrape off the hardened fat that rises to the top.

- To cut down on odors when cooking cabbage or cauliflower, add a little vinegar to the water and don't overcook.

- Three large stalks of celery, chopped and added to about two cups of beans (navy, brown, pinto, etc.), make the dish easier to digest.

- Fresh is best, but to reduce time in the kitchen, use canned or frozen broths or bouillon bases. Canned or frozen vegetables, such as peas, green beans, and corn, also work well.

- Ideally, cold soups should be served in chilled bowls.

- Perk up soggy lettuce by spritzing it with a mixture of lemon juice and cold water.

- You can easily remove egg shells from hard-boiled eggs if you quickly rinse the eggs in cold water after they are boiled. Add a drop of food coloring to help distinguish cooked eggs from raw ones.

- Your fruit salads will look better when you use an egg slicer to make perfect slices of strawberries, kiwis, or bananas.

- The ratio for a vinaigrette is typically 3 parts oil to 1 part vinegar.

- For salads, cook pasta al dente (slightly chewy to the bite). This allows the pasta to absorb some of the dressing and not become mushy.

- Fresh vegetables require little seasoning or cooking. If the vegetable is old, dress it up with sauces or seasoning.

- Chill the serving plates to keep the salad crisp.

- Fruit juices, such as pineapple and orange, can be used as salad dressing by adding a little olive oil, nutmeg, and honey.

SOUPS & SALADS

LOLA'S CLAM CHOWDER
Janice McWhorter

¼ lb. salt pork
2 c. onion
4 lg. potatoes
4 (10) cans clams, drain and keep
   liquid

1 ½ tsp. salt
1 tsp. Tabasco
4 c. half & half
3 c. milk
4 T. butter

In a large pot, cook salt pork; remove. Cook onion in fat. Add potatoes, clam liquid, salt and Tabasco (simmer until potatoes are cooked). Add remaining ingredients. Heat but do not boil.

TACO SOUP
Janice McWhorter

1 lb. ground beef and sm. onion,
   brown
3 c. water
1 can chile beans
1 can white corn
1 can diced tomatoes with peppers

1 (4-oz.) can diced Ortega chilies
1 pkg. dry Ranch dressing
1 pkg. taco seasoning
1 can pinto beans, rinsed and
   drained
1 can stewed tomatoes

Mix; simmer 30 minutes in pot or 2 hours in crockpot.

MINESTRONE SOUP
Janice McWhorter

Season 1 pound of ground beef, ½ bell pepper, ½ onion and 1 stalk celery, brown in skillet. In large pot, add:

1 qt. water
2 c. beef broth
1 tsp. oregano
Meat
1 T. parsley

¼ tsp. pepper
2 lg. carrots
½ tsp. basil
½ tsp. garlic salt

Simmer 20 minutes. Add:

1 (15-oz.) can garbanzo beans
1 (16-oz.) can green beans, drained
1 (15-oz.) can kidney beans

1 ¼ c. mostaccioli macaroni,
   uncooked

Cook 15 to 20 minutes, until macaroni is done.

SPINACH FRITTATA
Janice McWhorter

2 pkgs. frozen spinach, thaw
3 c. cottage cheese
6 to 7 T. flour
¾ cube butter or margarine

9 eggs, beaten
¾ lb. sharp cheddar cheese, grated
1 sm. grated onion

Mix. Bake in cookie sheet with sides 20 minutes at 350°. Perfect for brunch.

CHICKEN TORTILLA SOUP
Janice McWhorter

2 T. olive oil
1 lg. onion, chopped
2 med. carrots, finely chopped
2 T. minced garlic
3 c. chicken broth
1 (14-oz.) can diced tomatoes
1 c. mild picante sauce
1 (15-oz.) can Ranch-Style beans
1 (15-oz.) can black beans, drained
   and rinsed
1 c. whole kernel corn
1 tsp. cumin

½ tsp. pepper
½ tsp. oregano
½ tsp. chili powder
⅛ tsp. paprika
2 c. chopped cooked chicken
¼ c. chopped cilantro (add just
   before serving)
Sliced avocado (opt.)
Cheese (opt.)
Sour cream (opt.)
Tortilla chips (opt.)

VEGETABLE BEEF SOUP
Cherrie Patine

1 sm. roast or stew meat
1-lb. bag baby carrots
½ head cabbage
5 or 6 potatoes
1 can tomatoes

1 sm. onion
1 can green beans
1 can corn
2 cans tomato sauce

Cook meat, carrots, potatoes and onion until done. Add; cook cabbage and all other ingredients. Let simmer until all ingredients are done. Serve. Makes a large pot.

TACO SOUP
Kelly Edwards

1 lb. ground beef
1 onion, chopped (1 prefer red)
1 pkg. taco seasoning
1 ½ c. water

15-oz. can kidney beans, drained
15-oz. can stewed tomatoes
8-oz. can tomato sauce
Tortilla chips

Toppings:

Grated cheese
Chopped olives
Chopped tomatoes

Avocados, cubed
Sour cream

Brown ground beef and onion in skillet. Combine ground beef mixture with taco seasoning, water, kidney beans, stewed tomatoes and tomato sauce in a saucepan (you can use crockpot) and simmer 1 to 2 hours. To serve, crumble tortilla chips into individual bowls and pour soup mixture over chips. Top with favorite toppings.

126207-15

FASTEST CHUNKY TOMATO CREAM SOUP

1 T. olive oil
½ c. chopped Vidalia onion
8 to 10 sprigs fresh thyme
1 tsp. sweet paprika
1 serrano pepper, seeded and
  chopped
Kosher salt and freshly ground
  black pepper

2 cloves garlic, smashed
1 T. plus 1 tsp. tomato paste
8 Roma tomatoes, cut into big
  chunks
1 qt. chicken stock
½ c. heavy cream, room temp.

In a stock pot over medium heat, combine olive oil, onion, thyme, paprika, serrano pepper, a pinch of salt and a few grinds of black pepper. Stir with a wooden spoon and cook until onion is tender but not browned, 5 to 8 minutes. Add garlic and tomato paste, stirring to coat everything in pot. Cook, stirring, over medium heat until paste turns a deep red, 8 to 10 minutes more. Add tomato chunks and bring to a simmer. Cook, stirring to ensure that a bit of moisture evaporates but tomatoes don't burn. Cook this way until tomatoes are tender and skins are peeling off, about 5 minutes. Add chicken stock and bring to a boil, then reduce to a simmer and cook for just 10 more minutes. Remove pot from heat and using tongs, remove thyme. Using an immersion blender, blitz soup in pot, leaving a few chunks of tomato for texture. Return to low heat and slowly stir in cream. Serve warm. Makes 4 to 6 servings.

BEEF & CABBAGE SOUP   *Wilma*

1 lb. ground beef
¾ c. diced onion
2 (16-oz.) cans pinto or red kidney
  beans
4 c. beef broth
1 (5-oz.) can tomato juice
2 (14½-oz.) cans crushed tomatoes

1 T. chili powder or taco seasonings
½ tsp. ground cumin
1 c. dried sm. shell-shaped pasta
½ med. head green cabbage,
  chopped
Salt to taste
1 tsp. black pepper

In a large skillet, cook beef and onion until beef is no longer pink and onion is translucent, breaking up beef as it cooks. Drain. In a large pot or Dutch oven, combine beef and remaining ingredients. Over medium heat, bring mixture to a boil. Cover and cook until pasta and cabbage are tender, about 15 minutes. Makes at least 8 servings. (It makes more servings, I guess we don't make as large servings.) Enjoy.

BEAN SOUP

2 cans pinto beans
1 can navy beans
1 c. Great Northern beans
1 bell pepper
1 med. onion

1 lb. ground beef
1 can Ro-Tel tomatoes
1 can water
2 T. ketchup
Salt to taste

Brown beef, onion and bell pepper. Drain. Salt to taste. Add beans and ketchup. Simmer until heated thoroughly.

SHOE PEG SALAD

Lucy Bowen

1 can shoe peg corn, white
1 can green peas
1 can French-style green beans
1 bell pepper, green or yellow, diced

4 oz. pimentos, diced
1 sm. purple onion, diced
Black olives, sliced (opt.)
1 c. Italian salad dressing or more

Drain vegetables. Add all ingredients and dressing. Marinate overnight. Keeps well in refrigerator.

LAYERED TACO SALAD

Betty Nickels
Tampa, FL

1 lb. lean ground beef (90% lean)
2 T. reduced sodium taco seasoning
1 c. salsa
1 T. lime juice
6 oz. baked tortilla chips (about 70 chips)
12 c. chopped iceberg lettuce
6 plum tomatoes, seeded and chopped

1 (15-oz.) can black beans, rinsed and drained
1½ c. (6 oz.) shredded reduced-fat Mexican cheese blend
1 lg. sweet yellow or red peppers, thinly sliced
1 med. red onion, thinly sliced
½ c. fat-free sour cream

In a large nonstick skillet, cook beef over medium heat 6 to 8 minutes, or until no longer pink, breaking into crumbles; drain. Sprinkle taco seasoning over beef; stir to combine. In a small bowl, mix salsa and lime juice. Arrange tortilla chips on a serving platter; layer with next 6 ingredients, beef mixture, salsa mixture and sour cream. Serve immediately. Makes 6 servings.

COTTAGE CHEESE SALAD
(Dialysis Patient)

Robin Marshall

2 lbs. cottage cheese
1 (8-oz.) can crushed pineapple

1 (8 oz.) Cool Whip
1 (3-oz.) pkg. Jello, any flavor

Followed all together.

POTATO SALAD

Lucy Bowen

8 potatoes, boiled
4 eggs, boiled and chopped
4 pickles or relish
1 sm. jar pimentos, chopped

1 c. celery, chopped
1 sm. onion, chopped*
1 c. black olives, sliced

Let potatoes cool; peel and chop. Add rest of ingredients.

Dressing:

1 pt. sour cream
1 c. mayonnaise
3 T. lemon juice

1 tsp. salt
½ tsp. black pepper

Mix well and add to above ingredients. Chill. *Can use dehydrated onion. Can add mustard.

14

WATERGATE SALAD
Robin Marshall

1 (8 oz.) Cool Whip
1 box instant pistachio pudding
1 (20-oz.) can crushed pineapple
 and juice

1 c. mini marshmallows
½ c. chopped walnuts

Fold dry pudding into Cool Whip. Add pineapple and juice, marshmallows and walnuts. Refrigerate until ready to serve.

THOUSAND ISLAND DRESSING
Margie Smith

1 c. mayonnaise
⅓ c. chili sauce (Heinz)
1 lg. sweet pickle, chopped

1 tsp. dried chopped onion
1 hard-cooked egg, chopped fine
2 T. chopped black olives

CRAB SALAD
Robin Marshall

1 bag noodles
2 lbs. crab meat
1 T. lemon pepper

1 c. sour cream
1 c. celery
1 c. mayonnaise

Cook noodles. Let cool some, then add all together; refrigerate until cool.

TEXAS CAVIAR
(Black-eyed Pea Salad)
Lucy Bowen

1 lb. black-eyed peas or 2 to 3 cans
 black-eyed peas
½ c. green bell peppers, diced
⅔ c. pimentos, diced

⅓ c. onions, diced
½ c. celery, diced
1 c. Italian dressing

Cook black-eyed peas; drain or drain canned black-eyed peas. Add all ingredients and dressing. Refrigerate.

SEAFOOD SALAD
M. Smith

1 pkg. imitation crab
1 T. chopped black olives
1 T. finely chopped celery

1 T. finely chopped paprika
2 pinch of dill
½ c. mayonnaise

Chill for at least 1 hour. Can be doubled. Can add pasta.

USE WHATEVER YOU GOT SALAD
Joyce Goodwin

1 c. mushrooms, cut in chunks
1 c. purple onion, cut in chunks
1 c. cauliflower, cut in chunks
1 c. green or red pepper, cut in
 chunks

1 c. zucchini, cut in chunks
1 c. radishes and celery, cut in
 chunks

(continued)

Mix 1 envelope of Good Seasoning Italian salad dressing in plastic bowl with lid. Whatever you have in refrigerator will do just fine. Pour salad dressing over veggies. Put lid on and place in refrigerator. Turn over or shake once in a while until time to serve.

SPAGHETTI SALAD
Sandra Kester

1-lb. pkg. spaghetti, cooked and drained well
8-oz. bottle Wish-Bone Italian dressing

½ bottle Schilling's Salad Supreme
½ bell pepper, chopped (green and red)
½ red onion, chopped

Mix well and marinate in salad dressing overnight. Set out at room temperature before serving, 4 to 6 hours.

CORN CHOWDER
B. L. Montgomery

1½ T. butter
1 lg. onion, diced
4 med. potato, diced
1 (10 oz.) frozen corn in butter sauce

2 stalks celery, diced
1½ (10¾-oz.) cans chicken broth
Salt and pepper
2 c. milk

Heat butter in soup pot and sauté the onion and celery until tender but not brown, 4 minutes. Stir often. Add broth, potatoes and salt and pepper. Bring to a boil and then simmer until potatoes are tender. Add corn and milk. Boil until warmed to taste. Corn will be done by warm up.

PISTACHIO JELLO SALAD
Carolyn Hartsfield
Mary Bullock

1 pkg. each: lime and lemon pudding
2 c. boiling water
1 c. cottage cheese

1 (No. 2) can crushed pineapple
1 can Eagle Brand milk
1 can mayonnaise
1 c. chopped walnuts

Stir water and Jello until syrupy. Add Eagle Brand, cottage cheese and mayonnaise; mix well, then add pineapple and nuts.

MACARONI SALAD
Lucy Bowen

1 pkg. salad macaroni
1 c. celery, chopped
1 sm. onion, chopped

5 eggs, boiled and chopped
1 c. black olives, sliced
1 sm. jar pimentos, chopped

Dressing:

1 pt. sour cream
1 c. mayonnaise
4 tsp. lemon juice

1 tsp. salt
½ tsp. black pepper

Boil macaroni and drain well. Add other ingredients; mix well. Mix dressing well and chill. Mix salad well and dressing. Chill.

16

HOT GERMAN POTATO SALAD

Edna Welch

9 med. potatoes
1 ½ lbs. smoked or pre-cooked
  bratwurst
6 slices bacon
¾ c. chopped onions
2 T. all-purpose flour

1 tsp. salt
½ tsp. celery seed
⅛ tsp. pepper
¼ c. sugar
1 ⅓ c. water
⅔ c. cider vinegar

Cook potatoes in a saucepan with salted water until tender. Cut sausage into ½-inch slices. Sauté in skillet until browned. Drain potatoes; peel, cut in ¾-inch cubes. Add to sausages. Keep warm. Cook bacon until crisp. Crumble and set aside. Drain all but 3 tablespoons drippings. Sauté onions in drippings until tender. Stir in flour, salt, celery seed and pepper; blend well. Add sugar, water and vinegar. Bring to boil 2 minutes. Pour over potato mixture and stir gently to coat. Sprinkle with bacon and serve warm. Makes 12 to 14 servings.

POTATO CASSEROLE

Alice Banning

2-lb. pkg. cubed hash browns
½ c. margarine
1 can cream of chicken soup

1 pt. sour cream
½ c. chopped green onions
1 ½ c. shredded Cheddar cheese

Heat butter with soup. Add sour cream, onions and cheese to soup and stir in potatoes. Put in refrigerator overnight in 9 x 13-inch greased pan. Bake at 350° for 45 minutes. Mix 3 tablespoons melted butter, ½ cup cheese and 1 cup crushed corn flakes. Top onto casserole. Bake 30 minutes longer.

HOMEMADE RANCH DRESSING

Alice Banning

1 qt. mayonnaise
1 to 1 ½ c. buttermilk
1 tsp. dried parsley flakes
1 tsp. dehydrated onion flakes

1 tsp. salt
½ tsp. black pepper
¼ tsp. granulated sugar
1 tsp. Accent

Mix all ingredients in mixer. Keep refrigerated. Amount of buttermilk used is determined by how thick or thin you like your dressing. For blue cheese, just add desired amount of blue cheese crumbles.

PRETZEL SALAD

Peggy Hosman

1 c. stick pretzels
1 ½ sticks oleo or butter

3 T. sugar

Break pretzels in small pieces. Spread in 9 x 13-inch pan or dish. Melt 1 ½ sticks oleo or butter and 3 tablespoons sugar. Pour over pretzels. Bake in 350° oven for 8 minutes. Remove and cool and soften 8-ounce package of cream cheese. Spread over pretzels.

BROCCOLI SALAD
Rhonda Pierce

3 c. chopped broccoli
1 c. honey roasted sunflower seeds
1 bottle Hidden Valley coleslaw
   dressing
1 lb. cooked and crumbled bacon

¼ c. red onion, chopped
½ c. Roma tomatoes, chopped
½ c. shredded cheese
½ c. sliced olives

Clean broccoli and cut into bite-size pieces at amount and size you desire. In a large bowl, combine all ingredients except bacon bits. Mix well and refrigerate for 2 hours before serving.

GERMAN COLESLAW
Edna Welch

1 (4-lb.) head cabbage, shredded
1 med. onion, shredded
1 c. sugar
1 tsp. celery seed

1 tsp. dry mustard
¾ c. corn oil
1 T. sugar
1 c. vinegar

Combine shredded cabbage and onions. Sprinkle 1 cup sugar over the vegetables and slaw to stand. Combine the remaining ingredients in saucepan. Heat to boiling. Pour the hot mixture over the vegetables. Cool, refrigerate until serving. Serves 12.

SQUASH & FARRO SALAD

1 ½ lbs. diced fresh butternut
   squash (½ to ¾-inch pieces),
   from a peeled and seeded 2 ½-lb.
   squash
4 T. olive oil
1 tsp. salt
½ tsp. black pepper
1 sm. rotisserie chicken
1 ½ c. Nature's Earthly Choice
   parboiled farro

½ c. unsweetened dried cranberries
½ tsp. ground cumin
½ tsp. ground ginger
½ tsp. ground cinnamon
½ c. cider vinegar
2 tsp. Dijon mustard
1 tsp. honey
2 c. mixed baby kale, shredded
½ c. crumbled goat cheese
½ c. toasted walnuts, chopped

Heat oven to 450°. Toss diced squash with 2 tablespoons of the oil and ¼ teaspoon each of the salt and pepper and spread onto a large rimmed baking sheet. Roast at 450° for 20 minutes, stirring halfway through. Cool to room temperature. Meanwhile, remove and discard skin from chicken. Shred meat into pieces, discarding bones (you'll need 3 cups shredded chicken). Refrigerate roasted squash and chicken overnight. The next evening, combine farro, ½ teaspoon of the salt and 4½ cups water in a large pot. Bring to a boil. Boil for 10 minutes, then stir in dried cranberries. Boil for an additional 5 minutes; drain and rinse. In a small skillet, combine remaining ½ teaspoon each: salt and pepper, the cumin, ginger and cinnamon. Toast over medium heat for 1 minute. In a small bowl, whisk together vinegar, mustard, honey and remaining 2 tablespoons oil. Slowly whisk into skillet with seasonings. Remove from heat. Reheat squash and chicken in microwave for 2 minutes. Combine farro, squash, chicken and kale in a large serving bowl. Drizzle with dressing. Gently toss and sprinkle with goat cheese and walnuts. Serve at room temperature. Makes 6 servings. Preparation time: 25 minutes.

126207-15

TOMATO SOUP AND GRILLED CHEESE PANINI

3 lbs. plum tomatoes
2 cloves garlic
1 (14.5-oz.) can reduced-sodium
 vegetable broth
¼ c. basil leaves, plus 15 lg. leaves
 for sandwiches

¼ tsp. salt
¼ tsp. black pepper
10 slices whole grain bread
1 T. jarred basil pesto
8 oz. fresh mozzarella
1 lg. tomato

The night before cooking, core, halve and seed tomatoes. Thinly slice garlic and combine in a resealable bag with tomatoes. Refrigerate overnight. In the morning, combine tomatoes and garlic with broth and ¼ cup of the basil leaves in a 4½-quart slow cooker. Season with salt and pepper. Cover and cook on high for 6 hours or on low for 8 hours. Once soup is almost done, heat panini press. Place 5 slices of the bread on a work surface. Spread ½ teaspoon pesto on each slice. Cut mozzarella and tomatoes into 10 thin slices each. Place 2 slices on the mozzarella on bread. Add 3 basil leaves to each sandwich and top each with 2 slices tomato. Top with 5 remaining bread slices of tomato. Top with 5 remaining bread slices and coat both sides of sandwiches with nonstick cooking spray. Cook sandwiches in panini press for 3 minutes, 2 to 3 sandwiches per batch, until browned and cheese is melted. While sandwiches cook, ladle half the tomato mixture into a blender. Blend until smooth. Add remaining tomato mixture to blender if there is space, or do in batches. Blend until smooth, or you can use an immersion blender instead. Divide among 5 bowls, about 1½ cups per serving. Serve with a sandwich. Makes 5 servings. Preparation time: 20 minutes.

HOT CHICKEN SALAD   *Kelly Edwards*

2 c. cooked cubed chicken or turkey
½ tsp. salt
2 T. lemon juice
½ c. grated cheese

2 c. sliced celery
½ c. chopped toasted almonds
2 tsp. grated onion

Combine all ingredients except cheese and potato chips and toss lightly. Pile lightly into casserole dish and sprinkle with grated cheese and potato chips. Bake at 450° for 15 minutes. Serves 4 to 6 people.

BEST CHINESE CHICKEN SALAD   *Kelly Edwards*

1 head of cabbage
3 green onions
3 to 4 c. cooked chicken breasts
2 pkgs. Top Ramen (don't need
 seasonings)
2 T. sugar

3 T. apple cider vinegar
½ c. vegetable oil
1½ T. sesame oil
½ tsp. black pepper
1 tsp. salt

Mix sugar and vinegar. Add salt and pepper and sesame oil, then add vegetable oil. Set aside. Chop cabbage, green onions and chicken and mix with the oil mixture. Crush uncooked Top Ramen (without its seasonings), then add to your salad. Mix well and refrigerate. Compliments guaranteed!

TACO SALAD
Kelly Edwards

1 lb. hamburger
1-oz. pkg. taco seasoning
1 (15.5-oz.) can kidney beans, drained
1 lg. head lettuce
1 ½ c. Cheddar cheese

1 lg. tomato, chopped
⅔ c. Pace picante sauce
3 c. tortilla chips, broken
1 avocado, diced
Kraft Catalina dressing

Brown hamburger in saucepan; drain fat. Add package of seasoning and mix well. Add beans. Cover and keep warm over low heat. In a large salad bowl, tear lettuce leaves and add cheese tomato, avocado and chips. Pour meat and beans into salad mixture. Add picante sauce and Catalina dressing to desired moistness. Toss and serve with warm sourdough bread and mixed fruit.

BAYOU SEAFOOD CASSEROLE
Kelly Edwards

1 (8-oz.) pkg. cream cheese
1 stick butter/margarine
1 lb. shrimp, peeled
1 lg. onion, chopped
1 bell pepper, chopped
2 ribs celery, chopped
2 T. butter
1 can cream of mushroom soup

1 can mushrooms, drained
1 T. garlic salt
1 tsp. Tabasco
½ tsp. red pepper
1 pt. crab meat
¾ c. cooked rice
Sharp cheese, grated
Cracker crumbs

Melt cream cheese and butter in microwave. Mix well. Sauté shrimp, onion, bell pepper and celery in 2 tablespoons butter. Add to the first mixture. Add soup, mushrooms, seasonings, crab meat and rice. Mix well. Place in 2-quart casserole and top with cheese and cracker crumbs. Bake at 350° for 20 to 30 minutes, or until bubbly. Freezes well. Serves 8.

GREENS & GRAIN SALAD

1 (6-oz.) ctn. fat-free yogurt (not Greek)
2 T. white wine vinegar
⅓ c. chopped fresh dill
1 tsp. sugar
½ tsp. salt
¼ tsp. black pepper
1 c. frozen fully cooked wheat berries, such as Stahlbush Island Farms

1 c. cooked lentils, such as Melissa's
1 (8.8-oz.) pkg. cooked beets, such as Love Beets, diced
8 c. chopped butter lettuce
8 c. baby spinach
½ c. chopped unsalted pistachios
1 (6-oz.) can canned salmon, such as Wild Planet, drained (opt.)

In a large bowl, stir together yogurt, vinegar, dill, sugar, salt and pepper; set aside. Heat wheat berries in a microwavable bowl for 2 minutes; stir and heat 1 more minute, until thawed. Toss wheat berries, lentils, beets, lettuce, spinach and pistachio in bowl with dressing. Gently fold in salmon if desired. Makes 4 servings. Preparation time: 15 minutes.

126207-15

GRANDMOTHER'S CHOWDER
Dulyse Molnar

1 lb. ground beef
1 med. onion, chopped
12 med. potatoes, peeled and
  cubed
3 c. water
Salt and pepper to taste

2 c. whole milk
1 (15 ¼-oz.) can whole kernel corn,
  drained
2 tsp. dried parsley flakes
1 c. (8 oz.) sour cream

HOMEMADE RANCH DRESSING
Alice Banning

1 qt. mayonnaise
1 to 1 ½ c. buttermilk
1 T. dried parsley flakes
1 T. dehydrated onion flakes

1 scant tsp. salt
¼ tsp. black pepper
¼ tsp. granulated garlic
1 scant tsp. Accent

Mix all ingredients in mixer. Keep refrigerated. Amount of buttermilk used is determined by how thick or thin you like your dressing. For blue cheese, just add desired amount of blue cheese crumbles.

CLAM CHOWDER
Christal Montgomery

5 lbs. potatoes
1 lb. bacon
1 med. onion
1 qt. half & half

2 cans cooked clams
1 bottle clam juice
2 cubes chicken bouillon
5 lbs. potatoes, peeled and chopped

Just barely cover with salted water. Fry bacon and onions. Once potatoes are done cooking, do not drain. Add in bacon, onions, half & half, 2 cans of clams, 1 bottle of clam juice and 2 cubes of chicken bouillon. Salt and pepper to taste.

Recipe Favorites

126207-15

Vegetables & Side Dishes

Helpful Hints

- When preparing a casserole, make an additional batch to freeze for when you're short on time. Use within 2 months.

- To keep hot oil from splattering, sprinkle a little salt or flour in the pan before frying.

- To prevent pasta from boiling over, place a wooden spoon or fork across the top of the pot while the pasta is boiling.

- Boil all vegetables that grow above ground without a cover.

- Never soak vegetables after slicing; they will lose much of their nutritional value.

- Green pepper may change the flavor of frozen casseroles. Clove, garlic, and pepper flavors get stronger when frozen, while sage, onion, and salt become more mild.

- For an easy no-mess side dish, grill vegetables along with your meat.

- Store dried pasta, rice (except brown rice), and whole grains in tightly covered containers in a cool, dry place. Refrigerate brown rice and freeze grains if you will not use them within 5 months.

- A few drops of lemon juice added to simmering rice will keep the grains separated.

- When cooking greens, add a teaspoon of sugar to the water to help vegetables retain their fresh colors.

- To dress up buttered, cooked vegetables, sprinkle them with toasted sesame seeds, toasted chopped nuts, canned french-fried onions, grated cheese, or slightly crushed seasoned croutons.

- Soufflé dishes are designed with straight sides to help your soufflé rise. Ramekins work well for single-serve casseroles.

- A little vinegar or lemon juice added to potatoes before draining will make them extra white when mashed.

- To avoid toughened beans or corn, add salt midway through cooking.

- If your pasta sauce seems a little dry, add a few tablespoons of the pasta's cooking water.

- To prevent cheese from sticking to a grater, spray the grater with cooking spray before beginning.

VEGETABLES & SIDE DISHES

SPINACH CASSEROLE

Mary Davies

4 pkgs. (boxes) chopped frozen
    spinach
1 (8-oz.) pkg. Philadelphia cream
    cheese

2 cans cream of mushroom soup
2 sm. cans Durkee French fried
    onions

Cook spinach and drain. In a large bowl combine cream cheese (cut in small pieces), 2 soups and 1 can onions. Mix together and add warm spinach. Mix. Put into a 9 x 13-inch casserole and top with second can of onions. Bake at 350° for 15 to 20 minutes, uncovered, until it bubbles.

JANICE'S KILLER BEANS

Janice McWhorter

8 slices bacon crisp and crumbled
½ c. brown sugar
½ tsp. garlic powder
½ c. cider vinegar or red wine
    vinegar
1 (15-oz.) can green lima beans,
    drained
1 (15-oz.) can kidney beans,
    drained

4 lg. red onions, sliced
1 tsp. dry mustard
1 tsp. salt
2 (15-oz.) cans butter beans,
    drained
1 (15-oz.) can baked beans

Cook bacon in skillet. Sauté onions in bacon fat. Add sugar, spices and vinegar. Cover and simmer 20 minutes. Add beans and mix with bacon. Bake 1 hour at 350° or simmer in a crockpot 2 to 3 hours.

MARINATED CARROTS

Janice McWhorter

2 lbs. carrots, sliced, boiled and
    drained
1 c. sugar
1 T. prepared mustard
1 T. salt
1 sm. bell pepper

½ c. oil
¾ c. cider vinegar
1 T. Worcestershire sauce
1 T. black pepper
1 sm. onion

Mix together all ingredients except for the carrots and cook until sugar dissolves. Add small bell pepper and small onion, cut in small pieces. Pour over carrots in a dish. Refrigerate overnight.

FRIED GREEN BEANS

Janice Pelham
From the Neely's

Peanut oil for frying
1 c. all-purpose flour
1 c. beer

2 tsp. black pepper plus more for
    seasoning
1 lb. green beans, ends trimmed

(continued)

Preheat oil to 375°. Whisk the beer, flour, salt and pepper until smooth. Dip green beans into batter to coat, letting excess drip off. Fry in the peanut oil in batches, until they are golden and crisp. Remove from oil with a spider strainer to a paper towel-lined sheet tray. Sprinkle with salt and pepper to taste.

CHALLENGE BUTTER BALSAMIC & HERB-ROASTED POTATOES

½ stick of butter	2 tsp. garlic, minced or pressed
2 T. minced onions	2 tsp. fresh chopped rosemary
2 tsp. fresh thyme leaves	½ tsp. salt
¼ tsp. black pepper	2 lbs. sm. red potatoes, washed and
3 T. balsamic vinegar	quartered

Preheat oven to 400°. Melt butter in 9 x 13-inch baking pan in the preheating oven (this takes 3 to 5 minutes, so watch carefully). Remove pan from oven and stir in garlic, onions, rosemary and thyme. Roll potatoes in seasoned butter and place potatoes with skin side up in pan. Roast 15 to 20 minutes, until potatoes are slightly tender. Stir the potatoes to re-coat with butter mixture and continue cooking 10 to 15 minutes. Drizzle balsamic vinegar over potatoes. Season with salt and pepper. Return to oven for an additional 5 to 7 minutes. Serve warm. Serves 4 to 6.

STUFFING-STUFFED CABBAGE ROLLS

3 c. butter or margarine	2 c. chopped onion
¼ c. chopped celery	1 c. diced ham
1 c. chicken broth	1 lg. cabbage leaves
1 c. corn bread stuffing	1 ½ tsp. dried basil, crushed
1 ½ c. tomato sauce	

Preheat oven to 350°. Lightly spray a shallow baking pan with nonstick cooking spray and set aside. Place the butter or margarine in a large skillet and melt over medium heat. Add the onion and celery and sauté for 5 minutes, or until the vegetables are soft but not browned. Add the ham and cook for 3 additional minutes, or until the ham is lightly browned. Stir in the chicken broth. Place the stuffing mix in a large bowl. Add the ham mixture and toss well to combine. Set aside. Place 3 quarts of water and 1 tablespoon of salt in a large pot and bring to a boil. Add the cabbage leaf, lower the heat and simmer for 5 minutes, or until the leaves have softened. Carefully remove the leaves and drain well. To make the rolls, place a cabbage leaf on a flat surface. Divide the stuffing mixture until you have 8, covering completely with the cabbage leaves. Place in baking dish and bake at 350° for about 20 minutes. Serves 4.

126207-15

SPICY THAI VEGETABLES

3 T. reduced sodium soy sauce
2 T. lime juice
1 T. fish sauce
2 tsp. sugar
6 baby bok choy (about 1 ½ lbs.),
sliced in half lengthwise, stems
end left intact
1 lg. bunch scallions, trimmed
2 c. red, orange and yellow grape
tomatoes

4 oz. sugar snap peas
Hot chili oil (opt.)
2 T. canola oil
1 T. chopped fresh ginger
1 T. chopped lemon grass
1 red Thai chili or sm. serrano chili,
seeded and chopped
6 red Thai chilies (opt.)
Lime wedges for squeezing
Thai basil (opt.)

In a mini chopper, combine soy sauce, oil, lime juice, fish sauce, ginger, lemon grass, sugar and chopped Thai chili or serrano. Whirl to blend. Place in a dish with bok choy, scallions and whole Thai chilies if using. Marinate 15 minutes. Heat a gas grill to medium high or the coals in a charcoal grill to medium hot. Lightly grease grates. Remove vegetables from marinade and reserve remaining liquid. Grill bok choy for about 4 minutes pr side and scallions and chilies (if using) for 2 to 3 minutes per side. Remove to platter. Place a grilling grid on grill and heat for a few minutes. Grill tomatoes and sugar snap peas on grid for about 5 minutes, turning frequently. Remove to platter with other vegetables, drizzle with reserved marinade. Serve with lime wedges for squeezing and, if desired, hot chili oil. Garnish with Thai basil, if desired. Serves 6.

TANDOORI GRILLED VEGETABLES
WITH MINT RAITA

1 c. plain Greek yogurt
2 T. chopped fresh ginger
1 clove garlic, chopped
1 tsp. Garam Masala
1 tsp. paprika
1 sm. head broccoli, cut into lg.
florets
2 med. firm ripe tomatoes, cut into
8 wedges
1 lg. yellow onion, cut into 16
wedges

8 wood skewers, soaked in cold
water for at least 1 hour
Grilled naan bread (opt.)
2 T. lemon juice
1 T. canola oil
1 tsp. salt
1 tsp. turmeric
¼ tsp. cayenne pepper
½ cauliflower, cut into lg. florets

In a large bowl, combine yogurt, lemon juice, ginger, oil, garlic, salt, Garam Masala, turmeric, paprika and cayenne. Whisk until smooth. Set aside. Bring a large pot of lightly salted water to a boil. Add broccoli and cauliflower. Simmer for 2 minutes. Drain and run under cold water. Pat dry. Add broccoli, cauliflower, tomato and onion to yogurt mixture; stir gently to coat. Cover and refrigerate for 30 minutes. Heat a gas grill to medium-high or the coals in a charcoal grill to medium-hot. Lightly grease grates. Alternately thread broccoli, cauliflower, tomato wedges and onion into wood skewers. Grill for about 2 to 3 minutes per side, until lightly charred. Remove to a serving platter. Serve with Mint Raita and if desired grilled naan. Serves 8. **Mint Raita:** In a small bowl, combine 1 cup plain Greek yogurt, ¼ peeled seedless cucumber, shredded, 3 tablespoons chopped fresh mint, 1 teaspoon lemon juice and ⅛ teaspoon salt. Cover and refrigerate until serving.

POTATO CASSEROLE

Arletta Renshaw

2 (28-oz.) bags O'Brien potatoes
1 (10.5-oz.) can garlic cream of
   mushroom soup or just cream of
   mushroom soup and ½ can water

1 (8-oz.) bag colby and Monterey
   cheese, finely shredded
2 c. chopped ham
Garlic, salt and pepper to taste

In a bowl, mix soup and the ½ can of water; mix together. Put potatoes in large bowl. Add half the bag of cheese, soup, ham, garlic, salt and pepper; mix well. Spray a 13 x 9-inch pan with Pam. Pour mix into pan. Bake at 325° for 45 minutes, covered with foil. Remove pan. Take off foil and add the rest of the cheese. Re-cover and cook for 45 more minutes. Remove foil and put the pan back in the oven and cook for about 20 more minutes.

LOADED BAKED POTATOES
(Diabetic)

4 (5- to 6-oz.) baking potatoes
1 (10-oz.) pkg. frozen broccoli in 1
   c. low fat cottage cheese

Cheese sauce

Prick potatoes with a fork. Microwave potatoes until tender. Using a knife, cut an X in the top of each potato. Press in and up the ends of each potato. Microwave broccoli according to package directions. Spoon cottage cheese onto potato and add broccoli with cheese sauce.

ASSORTED VEGETABLE PLATTER

3 T. pomegranate balsamic vinegar
½ tsp. salt
6 T. canola oil
1 T. chopped parsley
1 lb. asparagus, trimmed
8 oz. baby carrots, halved
   lengthwise
3 T. honey
¼ tsp. black pepper
1 T. chopped fresh sage

1 tsp. chopped rosemary
1 med. eggplant (1 lb.), cut into ½-
   inch slices
1 lg. summer squash, cut into ½-
   inch slices
1 red pepper, seeded and cut into
   ½-inch strips
2 lg. shallots, peeled and cut into 8
   pieces

In a small bowl, whisk together vinegar, honey, ¼ teaspoon of the salt and the black pepper. Gradually whisk in oil; add sage, parsley and rosemary. Set aside. Heat a gas grill to medium-high or the coals in a charcoal grill to medium-hot. Lightly grease grates. Brush vegetables with dressing. Grill for about 5 minutes per side, until crisp tender. Brush with additional dressing and turn as needed to prevent burning. Cook in batches if necessary. Serves 6.

GINGER GLAZED CARROTS

¼ c. butter
1 T. grated or finely minced fresh
   gingerroot

½ tsp. ground ginger
¼ c. brown sugar
1 ½ lbs. whole baby carrots (4 c.)

(continued)

Melt butter in a large fry pan over medium heat. Add sugar and honey and heat until bubbly. Stir in minced gingerroot and ground ginger. Add carrots and bring to a boil. Reduce heat and simmer, covered, for about 10 minutes, or until carrots are cooked. Remove the lid from the pan and continue to simmer for 5 minutes, stirring to coat the carrots as the sauce is reduced. Stir in ¼ teaspoon salt to taste.

CREAMED SPINACH CASSEROLE

1 (10-oz.) pkg. frozen chopped spinach
½ tsp. salt
½ c. shredded cheddar cheese
½ c. milk

5 T. butter or margarine, divided
¼ tsp. pepper
2 eggs
¼ c. soft bread crumbs

In a saucepan, cook spinach in a small amount of water for 2 to 3 minutes; drain thoroughly. Add 4 tablespoons butter, salt, pepper, cheese, eggs and milk. Spoon into 2 greased 8-ounce baking dishes. Melt the remaining butter. Add crumbs. Sprinkle over spinach mixture. Bake, uncovered, at 350° for 20 to 25 minutes, or until almost set.

CHEESY POTATO CASSEROLE

2 eggs
½ c. chopped onions
¼ c. dry bread crumbs
¼ tsp. pepper
4 bacon strips, cooked and crumbled

2 med. potatoes, peeled and grated
½ tsp. salt
¾ c. shredded cheddar cheese

In a medium bowl, beat eggs. Stir in potatoes, onion, crumbs, salt and pepper. Pour into a greased 1-quart baking dish. Bake at 350° for 30 minutes, or until potatoes are tender. Top with cheese and bacon; return to oven for 5 to 7 minutes, until cheese is melted. Serves 2.

UNUSUAL CORN CASSEROLE

1 egg
1 stick melted butter
1 can cream-style corn

1 c. dairy sour cream
1 c. whole kernel corn, drained
1 (8-oz.) pkg. corn muffin mix

Beat egg. In following order, stir in sour cream, melted butter, cream-style corn, kernel corn and corn muffin mix. Pour into buttered baking dish. Bake in a 350° oven for 45 minutes.

PEAR & PECAN STUFFED SQUASH

4 acorn squash, halved lengthwise
and seeded
2 T. plus 1 tsp. olive oil
1 c. cooked wheat berries
⅓ c. roughly chopped pecans
¼ tsp. pepper
1 (10-oz.) bag frozen kale, drained
and rinsed
¾ tsp. salt
1 pear, peeled, cored and diced into
sm. cubes
½ c. shredded Parmesan
2 tsp. chopped sage
4 garlic cloves, chopped
1 (15.5-oz.) can butter beans
1 tsp. lemon juice

Heat oven to 400°. Coat squash halves with 2 tablespoons of the olive oil. Sprinkle cavities with ¼ teaspoon of the salt. Place, cut side down, on 2 baking sheets (4 halves on each sheet). Roast for 30 minutes. Let cool slightly and scoop flesh out of 4 of the 8 halves and discard skins; place in a resealable container. Turn on broiler. In a microwavable bowl, combine cooked wheat berries, pear, ¼ cup of the Parmesan, the pecans, sage and ¼ teaspoon of the pepper. Microwave for 1 minute. Carefully fill remaining 4 squash halves with mixture. Sprinkle with remaining ¼ cup Parmesan and broil on high for 2 to 3 minutes, until cheese is melted and lightly browned. Meanwhile, in a medium pot, heat remaining 1 teaspoon olive oil over medium heat. Stir in garlic; cook 1 minute. Mix in frozen kale and ½ cup water; bring to a boil. Cover and cook 3 minutes. Stir in butter beans, lemon juice, remaining ¼ teaspoon salt and remaining ⅛ teaspoon pepper. Cook 2 minutes, until beans are heated. Serve with squash. Makes 4 servings. Preparation time: 20 minutes.

CHUNKY BAKED POTATOES   *Rhonda Pierce*

6 to 8 potatoes
Parmesan cheese, shredded
⅓ c. oil
Real bacon bits

Peel and slice potatoes. Cut into ⅛ size or smaller (like thick French fries) and put in baking pan or cookie sheet. Put oil, salt and pepper over potatoes and mix thoroughly, getting on all potatoes. Cook for 40 minutes at 450°, stirring occasionally, until brown. On the last 10 minutes, sprinkle Parmesan cheese and bacon bits over potatoes.

DILL-SAUCED PEAS

2 T. butter or margarine, melted
2 tsp. cornstarch
1 tsp. instant chicken-flavored
bouillon
¼ tsp. onion salt
⅛ tsp. white pepper
1 (16-oz.) can peas
½ c. dairy sour cream
½ tsp. dill

Blend together butter, cornstarch, bouillon, onion salt and pepper in a saucepan. Drain peas, reserving ¼ cup liquid. Add reserved liquid to saucepan; stir until smooth. Cook over moderate heat, stirring constantly, until slightly thickened. Add sour cream and dill. Stir in peas, heat to serving temperature but do not boil. Serves 4.

126207-15

CHEESE-STUFFED POTATOES

6 baking potatoes
Corn oil
3 T. butter or margarine
¼ c. chopped onion
2 tsp. original Worcestershire sauce

½ tsp. salt
¾ c. shredded sharp Cheddar
  cheese
Paprika (opt.)

Brush potatoes lightly with oil; place on a baking sheet. Bake in preheated 400° oven until potatoes are tender, about 1 hour. Cut potatoes in half lengthwise. Carefully scoop out potato from skins. Mash potato with butter, onion, Worcestershire sauce and salt. Spoon mashed potato mixture into potato shells. Top with cheese. Return to hot oven and bake until cheese is melted, about 15 minutes. Sprinkle with paprika if desired. Serves 6.

QUICK PEA MEDLEY

2 T. butter or margarine
¼ c. chopped onion
¼ c. chopped green pepper
1 (10-oz.) pkg. frozen peas

1 (8¼-oz.) can tomatoes, broken up
1½ tsp. original Worcestershire
  sauce
½ tsp. salt

Melt butter in a medium-size saucepan. Add onion and green pepper; sauté 3 minutes. Add peas, tomatoes, Worcestershire sauce and salt. Mix gently. Bring to a boil. Reduce heat and simmer, uncovered, 5 minutes. Serves 4.

POTATOES AU GRATIN

4 c. thinly sliced peeled potatoes
¾ c. minced onion
¾ tsp. salt
1 (10¾-oz.) can condensed
  Cheddar cheese soup

½ c. milk
1 T. original Worcestershire sauce

Arrange potatoes, onions and salt in alternate layers in a well buttered 2-quart casserole. Repeat 3 times. Heat soup, milk and Worcestershire sauce in a saucepan. Pour over potato mixture. Cover and bake in preheated 375° oven for 45 minutes. Remove cover; bake 15 minutes longer. Serves 6.

POTATO PATTIES

2 c. seasoned mashed potatoes
1 egg or 2 egg yolks, slightly
  beaten

1 T. minced onion
1 T. chopped green pepper
2 T. corn oil

Combine all ingredients except oil; mix well. Shape into 6 patties. Brown well in oil, about 4 minutes on each side.

RED CABBAGE WITH APPLES

¼ c. margarine
½ c. chopped onion
3 lbs. red cabbage, shredded (3 qt.)
⅓ c. light corn syrup
2 T. cider vinegar

1 T. salt
1 c. Burgundy wine
2 tart apples, peeled, cored and
   sliced
1 c. red currant jelly

Melt margarine in 5-quart Dutch oven over medium-high heat, add onion and cook 3 minutes, stirring frequently, or until tender. Add cabbage, corn syrup, vinegar and salt. Cook, stirring occasionally, 15 minutes. Stir in wine; bring to a boil. Reduce heat and simmer 30 minutes, or until cabbage is tender. Add apples and jelly; stir until jelly is melted. Simmer 15 minutes longer. Serves 8 to 10.

HOT CABBAGE SLAW

⅓ c. water
2 beef bouillon cubes
1 med. size (about ½ lb.) green
   cabbage, coarsely shredded
½ c. chopped onion

½ c. grated carrot
2 T. wine vinegar
2 tsp. original Worcestershire sauce
½ tsp. caraway seed

Combine water and bouillon cubes in a large saucepan. Bring to a boil, stirring to dissolve bouillon cubes. Add cabbage; reduce heat and simmer, covered, 10 minutes. Add remaining ingredients; simmer, covered, until cabbage is tender, about 10 minutes longer. Serves 6.

GERMAN SWEET & SOUR RED CABBAGE

4 T. butter
8 c. shredded red cabbage
¼ c. sherry
1 tsp. salt
⅛ tsp. pepper
1 c. minced onion

2 T. sugar
⅓ c. peeled and grated tart apples
¼ c. white raisins, soaked 45
   minutes in cold water, then
   drained
1 c. currant jelly

Melt butter in a skillet over medium heat. Add remaining ingredients except jelly; stir well. Cover, reduce heat and simmer 40 minutes. Add jelly; cover and simmer 20 minutes longer. Serves 8.

CARROTS, SWEET & SOUR

1 ½ lbs. whole baby carrots, peeled
   and trimmed
⅓ c. honey
⅓ c. fresh lemon juice
1 c. slivered red or green bell
   pepper
⅛ tsp. cardamom

⅛ tsp. cloves
⅛ tsp. cinnamon
⅛ tsp. ginger
⅛ tsp. seasoned salt
⅛ tsp. lemon pepper
1 ½ T. Marsala wine

(continued)

126207-15

Parboil carrots in water until almost tender; drain. Combine remaining ingredients to make a glazed sauce. Cook carrots in sauce until tender and glazed, stirring occasionally. Serves 6.

BAKED STUFFED SWEET POTATOES

4 med. sweet potatoes	½ tsp. salt
¼ c. light corn syrup	Dash of ground cinnamon
¼ c. margarine, melted	

Pierce each potato once with a fork; place on a cookie sheet. Bake in preheated 400° oven 1 hour, or until tender. Cut an oval in the top of each potato with a sharp knife, scoop out potatoes, reserving skins. Mash potatoes in a bowl. Add corn syrup, margarine and salt; stir until smooth. Spoon potato mixture into skins; sprinkle with cinnamon. Bake in preheated 350° oven 15 minutes, or until heated through. Serves 4.

CANDIED SWEET POTATOES

1 c. dark corn syrup	2 T. margarine
½ c. firmly packed dark brown	12 med. sweet potatoes, cooked,
sugar	peeled and halved lengthwise

Bring corn syrup, brown sugar and margarine to a boil over medium heat in a small saucepan; reduce heat and simmer 5 minutes. Pour ½ cup syrup into 13 x 9 x 2-inch baking dish. Arrange potatoes in syrup; top with remaining syrup. Bake in preheated 350° oven, basting often, 20 minutes, or until well glazed. Serves 12.

LOADED BAKED POTATOES
(Diabetic)

Lucy Bowen

4 (5- to 6-oz.) baking potatoes	1 c. low fat cottage cheese
1 (10-oz.) pkg. frozen broccoli in	
cheese sauce	

Prick potatoes with a fork. Microwave potatoes until tender. Using a knife, cut an X in the top of each potato. Press in and up on the ends of each potato. Microwave broccoli according to package directions. Spoon cottage cheese onto potato and add broccoli/cheese sauce.

SWEET POTATO CASSEROLE

Alice Banning

Spray pan with Pam.

3 c. mashed sweet potatoes, baked	1 tsp. vanilla
until very soft, not canned	½ c. butter (1 cube)
½ c. sugar	2 eggs
⅓ c. milk	

Pour mixture into a casserole dish; do not cover.

(continued)

Topping:

1 c. light brown sugar	⅓ c. flour
⅓ c. butter, not melted	1 c. pecans or walnuts

Sprinkle on top. Bake at 350° for 25 to 30 minutes, until hot and browned on top.

BROCCOLI CHEESE BAKE
Alice Hopfe

2 pkgs. frozen broccoli florets, defrosted	Pinch of salt and pepper
	8 oz. shredded cheese
1 (12 oz.) cottage cheese	3 eggs
3 ½ T. flour	½ c. butter

Mix together and bake at 350° for 1 hour, covered.

AWESOME MASHED POTATOES

5 lbs. white potatoes, pared	8 oz. sour cream
8 oz. cream cheese	2 T. garlic salt

Boil potatoes until tender. Drain. Whip thoroughly with remaining ingredients. Place in greased casserole dish. Bake at 375° for 1 hour. Serve hot. This dish may be made ahead and refrigerated until 1 hour before serving. Serves 12.

FRIED OKRA
Rhonda Pierce

1 lb. okra, washed and drained	½ tsp. pepper
1 c. yellow corn meal	1 tsp. salt
½ c. flour	Vegetable oil

Cut off and discard stem end from each okra pod. Set okra pods aside. Mix together flour, cornmeal, salt and pepper. Meanwhile, heat about ½ to 1 inch of vegetable oil or bacon grease in a saucepan or skillet (I prefer iron skillet) to a medium to high temperature. Bread okra in flour mixture. Fry okra until golden brown on all side, turning frequently. **Tip:** If you want okra more breaded, you can add 1 egg and ¼ cup of milk to mixture with okra. Beat egg slightly, then add milk and egg to mixture, covering okra thoroughly before putting in skillet.

BROCCOLI CASSEROLE
Lucy Bowen

1 pkg. frozen chopped broccoli	1 egg, beaten
½ can cream of mushroom soup	½ c. grated cheddar cheese
1 sm. onion, chopped	

Combine and put in 9 x 9-inch dish. Sprinkle bread crumbs on top. Bake at 350° for 30 minutes.

126207-15

PICKLED OKRA

Joyce Goodwin

For 6 pints:

6 T. salt
3 c. water
1 T. mustard seed
3 c. white vinegar

1 tsp. dill
18 peppercorns
1 sm. red pepper (hot) in each jar

Divide mustard seed, dill and peppercorns into the 6 jars. Pack jars with okra. In a saucepan, bring water, vinegar and water to boil. Add to packed jars, seal with lids and put in water, covering ⅔ of jar and boil for 10 minutes.

LEFTOVER MASHED POTATOES

2 eggs
1 heaping c. cheddar cheese
2 T. chopped chives
3 c. mashed potatoes

⅓ c. sour cream plus more for
  serving
2 T. grated Parmesan cheese
Salt and pepper to taste

Preheat oven to 400°. Butter 8 or 9 wells in cupcake pan. In a medium mixing bowl, whisk eggs, then add sour cream, both cheeses and chives. Taste the mashed potatoes to see if they need more salt and pepper. Add to taste. Add potatoes to bowl; mix well. Spoon into pan, filling cups just to the top or just a little below. Bake 25 to 35 minutes, or until they pull away from sides of cups and are golden brown all over. Remove from oven. Cool for 5 minutes. Turn over onto a platter. Serve with sour cream.

RICE (SPANISH)

1 c. rice
1 c. tomato sauce
2 c. water

1 pkg. chicken bouillon with tomato
  granules

Sauté rice in oil until browned. Add other ingredients. Cook until tender.

GINGER GLAZED CARROTS

¼ c. (½ stick) butter
¼ c. brown sugar
1 T. honey
1 T. grated or finely minced fresh
  gingerroot

½ tsp. ground ginger
1 ½ lbs. whole baby carrots (4 c.)
¼ tsp. salt or to taste

Melt butter in large fry pan over medium heat. Add sugar and honey and beat until bubbly. Stir in minced gingerroot and ground ginger. Add carrots and bring to a boil. Reduce heat and simmer, covered, for about 10 minutes, or until carrots are cooked. Remove the lid from the pan and continue to simmer for 5 minutes, stirring to coat the carrots as the sauce is reduced. Stir in ¼ teaspoon salt to taste.

SCALLOPED POTATOES

Alice Banning

3 c. sliced potatoes
8 slices bacon
1 lg. onion, chopped

2 cans cheddar cheese soup
1 cube margarine
¾ c. canned milk

Melt and heat butter, cheese soup and milk. Combine all ingredients in dish. Save and top with some bacon. Cook at 350° for 1½ to 2 hours.

UNUSUAL CORN CASSEROLE

Edna Welch

1 egg
1 c. dairy sour cream
1 stick butter, melted

1 c. whole kernel corn, drained
1 c. canned cream-style corn
1 (8½-oz.) pkg. corn muffin mix

Beat egg. In following order, stir in sour cream, melted butter, cream-style corn, kernel corn and corn muffin mix. Pour into a buttered baking dish. Bake in a 350° oven for 45 minutes.

126207-15

Main Dishes

Helpful Hints

- Certain meats, like ribs and pot roast, can be parboiled before grilling to reduce the fat content.

- Pound meat lightly with a mallet or rolling pin, pierce with a fork, sprinkle lightly with meat tenderizer, and add marinade. Refrigerate for 20 minutes and cook or grill for a quick and succulent meat.

- Marinating is a cinch if you use a plastic bag. The meat stays in the marinade and it's easy to turn. Cleanup is easy; just toss the bag.

- It's easier to thinly slice meat if it's partially frozen.

- Adding tomatoes to roasts naturally tenderizes the meat as tomatoes contain an acid that works well to break down meats.

- Whenever possible, cut meat across the grain; this will make it easier to eat and also give it a more attractive appearance.

- When frying meat, sprinkle paprika on the meat to turn it golden brown.

- Thaw all meats in the refrigerator for maximum safety.

- Refrigerate poultry promptly after purchasing. Keep it in the coldest part of your refrigerator for up to 2 days. Freeze poultry for longer storage. Never leave poultry at room temperature for over 2 hours.

- When frying chicken, canola oil provides a milder taste, and it contains healthier amounts of saturated and polyunsaturated fats. Do not cover the chicken once it has finished cooking because covering will cause the coating to lose its crispness.

- One pound of boneless chicken equals approximately 3 cups of cubed chicken.

- Generally, red meats should reach 160° and poultry should reach 180° before serving. If preparing fish, the surface of the fish should flake off with a fork.

- Rub lemon juice on fish before cooking to enhance the flavor and help maintain a good color.

- Scaling a fish is easier if vinegar is rubbed on the scales first.

- When grilling fish, the rule of thumb is to cook 5 minutes on each side per inch of thickness. For example, cook a 2-inch thick fillet for 10 minutes per side. Before grilling, rub with oil to seal in moisture.

MAIN DISHES

CHICKEN DELICIOUS
Kelly Edwards

1 can cream of celery soup and 1
  can cream of mushroom soup
1 c. Best Foods mayonnaise
1 can sliced water chestnuts

4 chicken breasts
1 pkg. Stove Top stuffing
¾ cube butter, melted

Boil chicken breasts for 45 minutes. Cut into small pieces. Mix soups, mayonnaise and water chestnuts together. Layer a 9 x 13-inch baking dish with chicken, then pour the soup mixture. Sprinkle dressing on top and pour butter over. Bake at 350° for 40 minutes.

HEARTY CHICKEN POT PIE
Lilly, Suzzie & Cherrie Moore

1 (10¾-oz.) can condensed chicken
  broth
1 ⅓ c. water, divided
4 med. carrots, thinly sliced (about
  1 ½ c.)
3 med. red potatoes, scrubbed and
  diced (about 1 ½ c.)
2 T. olive oil

2 c. quartered med. mushrooms
1 med. onion, coarsely chopped
1 c. frozen peas
⅓ c. all-purpose flour
1 refrigerated unbaked pie crust for
  9-inch pie
2 ½ c. chopped cooked chicken

Combine broth, 1 cup water, carrots and potatoes in a medium saucepan. Bring to a boil; reduce heat and simmer over low heat 10 minutes. Preheat oven to 425°. Heat oil in a large skillet over medium heat. Add mushrooms and onion; sauté until softened, about 5 minutes. Stir in broth mixture and peas. Whisk remaining ⅓ cup water into the flour until smooth; whisk into vegetable mixture. Increase heat to medium-high; bring to a boil. Spread out pie crust on floured surface. Measure and roll if necessary to fit 1 inch larger than top of a 2-quart shallow baking dish. Stir chicken into vegetable mixture and transfer to the baking dish. Place crust over filling; trim and flute edge. Cut a scalloped round from center with a cookie cutter. Bake until filling is bubbly and crust is browned, about 20 minutes.

RICE KRISPIE CHICKEN
Sandra Kester

1 chicken or whatever parts you
  prefer
½ box med. size Rice Krispies,
  crush fine

1 to 1 ½ c. margarine
Salt, pepper and garlic

Skin all parts of chicken (breasts and thighs). Melt margarine. Season chicken. Dip into margarine. Dip in Rice Krispies. Place on foil in cookie sheet. Bake at 350° for 45 minutes to 1 hour. **Do not** turn chicken while cooking. Good with cheesy potato casserole and corn on cob.

BEEFY CABBAGE BEAN STEW

½ lb. lean ground beef (90% lean)
3 c. shredded cabbage or angel hair coleslaw mix
1 (16-oz.) can red beans, rinsed and drained
1 (14 ½-oz.) can diced tomatoes, undrained
1 (8-oz.) can tomato sauce
¾ c. salsa or picante sauce
1 med. green pepper, chopped
1 sm. onion, chopped
3 garlic cloves, minced
1 tsp. ground cumin
½ tsp. pepper

In a large skillet, cook beef over medium heat for 4 to 6 minutes, or until it is no longer pink, breaking it into crumbles; drain. Transfer meat to a 4-quart slow cooker. Stir in remaining ingredients. Cook, covered, on low 6 to 8 hours, until cabbage is tender. Makes 6 servings. Preparation time: 20 minutes.

TACO MEAT LOAF

Diane Essinger
Findlay, OH

1 egg, beaten
½ c. sour cream
⅓ c. salsa
2 to 4 T. taco seasoning
1 c. crushed tortilla chips
½ c. shredded cheddar cheese
2 lbs. lean ground beef (90% lean)

Optional Toppings:

Sour cream
Salsa
Shredded cheddar cheese
Shredded lettuce
Sliced ripe olives

In a large bowl, combine the first 6 ingredients. Crumble beef over mixture and mix well. Pat into a 3-quart slow cooker. Cover and cook on low for 8 hours, or until no pink remains and a meat thermometer reads 160°. Top with optional ingredients if desired. Makes 8 servings. Preparation time: 10 minutes.

APPLE GLAZED PORK CHOP

Janice Pelham

½ c. Smucker's apple jelly
¼ tsp. ground allspice
1 tsp. ground cinnamon
⅛ tsp. ground cloves
2 sm. baking apples, cored and sliced
4 (1-inch thick) pork chops

Heat broiler. Combine jelly, allspice, cinnamon and cloves in saucepan. Cook over low heat, stirring occasionally, until jelly melts. Keep warm. Place pork chops on rack in broiler pan. Broil 5 inches from heat, 7 minutes on each side. Remove from oven. Brush one side with jelly glaze; broil 3 minutes. Flip and brush other side with glaze. Top with apple slices and drizzle with remaining glaze. Boil 3 minutes. Serve immediately. Makes 4 servings. Preparation time: 10 minutes.

MAY ROBISON'S PARTY TATERS & HAM

28 oz. Ore-Ida potatoes O'Brien
12 oz. Hormel cubed ham
10-oz. can cream of chicken
2 c. shredded cheese of your choice

(continued)

36

126207-15

Mix all ingredients together. in bowl, then place in buttered casserole dish. Bake in preheated 400° oven until cooked through and golden brown on top, about 25 minutes. Serve with sour cream.

POP'S HAMBURGER NOODLE CASSEROLE

Greg Cossel

1 to 1 ½ lbs. ground beef
12 to 18 egg noodles
1 (14.5-oz.) can diced tomatoes, Italian-style, or 2 (8-oz.) cans tomato sauce, Italian-style
1 (6-oz.) can tomato paste

1 (4-oz.) can diced Ortega chilies
½ diced sweet yellow onion
2 c. sharp cheddar cheese
8-oz. block cream cheese
1 c. sour cream
3 diced green onions

Add to taste:

1 ½ T. minced garlic
2 T. dried parsley
2 T. Italian seasoning

1 tsp. paprika
1 tsp. chili powder
Salt and pepper

Preheat oven to 350°. Add hamburger, Ortega chilies, sweet yellow onion and minced garlic in a nonstick skillet and brown. Drain off liquid and add diced tomatoes or tomato sauce, tomato paste, paprika, chili powder, salt and pepper. Let simmer while noodles are cooking. In a large bowl, add sour cream, cream cheese (room temperature), parsley and green onions. Bring salted water to a boil and add egg noodles. Cook about 10 minutes, or until al dente. When noodles are done, drain off the water and add noodles to the cream cheese/sour cream mixture. Mix until cream cheese is fully melted and smooth. In a 9 x 13-inch baking dish, add the hamburger. Put noodle mixture evenly over the top of the hamburger. Sprinkle 1 cup of the cheddar cheese over the top. Bake for 15 minutes, then add the other cup of cheddar cheese. Bake an additional 15 minutes, or until cheese is slightly browned.

SINGAPORE SHRIMP NOODLES

1 (7-oz.) pkg. vermicelli rice noodles, such as China Bowl
3 T. vegetable oil
3 T. low-sodium soy sauce
2 T. rice vinegar
2 T. curry powder
2 tsp. sesame oil
1 (1-inch) piece ginger, peeled and grated

1 clove garlic, grated
1 lb. frozen cooked, peeled and deveined shrimp, thawed
1 sweet red pepper, cored and thinly sliced
1 c. bean sprouts
1 jalapeño, thinly sliced
¼ c. cilantro, chopped

In a large bowl, cover rice noodles with 2 inches of very hot water. Soak for 10 minutes. Microwave for 2 minutes. Let cool slightly, then carefully remove noodles to a cutting board, reserving ¼ cup of the soaking liquid. Cut noodles into thirds. In the same bowl, whisk together reserved liquid, vegetable oil, soy sauce, vinegar, curry powder, sesame oil, ginger and garlic. Return noodles to bowl and toss with shrimp, red pepper, scallions, bean sprouts, jalapeño and cilantro. Makes 4 servings. Preparation time: 15 minutes.

ONE-POT CHILI

Arletta Renshaw

2 (40-oz.) cans pinto beans
1 ½ lbs. ground turkey or ground
  beef
1 can tomato juice
1 (4-oz.) can jalapeño peppers,
  juice and all (I like it hot)

Chili powder to taste
Salt and pepper to taste
1 med. onion
Garlic powder to taste

Cook onion in pot. Add and brown meat in large heavy pot. Season to taste. Add chili powder to taste. Add jalapeño chilies and beans. Add as much tomato juice as you want (I like a lot of juice). Simmer until onion is soft and chili powder is cooked in.

CHILI RELLENOS CASSEROLE

Arletta Renshaw

½ lb. ground beef
¼ onion
1 (10-oz.) can whole chilies
1 ½ c. cheese
2 eggs
¾ c. milk

⅛ c. flour
1 tsp. cumin
⅛ tsp. salt
½ tsp. pepper
1 (4-oz.) can diced green chilies

Preheat oven to 350°. Cook and drain hamburger. Add cumin, salt and pepper. Line bottom of 8 x 8-inch pan with chilies. Top with cheese and diced chilies. Whisk together eggs, milk, then flour. Mix well and pour over chilies and cheese. Bake 35 to 40 minutes.

MEXICAN LASAGNA CONPUERCO

3 lbs. ground beef
2 pkgs. taco seasoning
2 (8-oz.) cans tomato sauce
1 c. diced tomatoes
1 (4-oz.) can diced green chile

1 lg. ctn. ricotta cheese
2 eggs, beaten
4 flour tortillas (soft taco)
2 c. shredded Monterey Jack cheese
1 sm. can sliced olives

Cook beef. Add taco seasoning, tomatoes, tomato sauce and chile. Bring to a boil over medium heat. Reduce heat to low and cook, uncovered, 5 minutes. Mix ricotta cheese and eggs. Spray 10 x 15-inch baking dish. Spread half of meat on bottom of dish. Top with 2 tortillas. Spread one half of ricotta cheese on top. Top with one-half of Monterey Jack cheese. Repeat process. Top with rest of cheese. Cover with olives. Bake at 350° for 20 to 30 minutes.

MEAT LOAF

Janice Pelham

1 lb. ground beef
1 ¼ tsp. garlic salt
¼ tsp. ground black pepper
½ c. chopped onion
½ c. chopped bell pepper
1 egg, lightly beaten

8 oz. canned diced tomatoes with
  juice
½ c. quick-cooking oats or crushed
  soda crackers or bread crumbs,
  whatever you have handy

(continued)

126207-15

Topping:

3 to 4 strips bacon, uncooked
⅓ c. ketchup

2 T. brown sugar
1 T. prepared mustard

Preheat oven to 375°. Mix all meat loaf ingredients well and place in a baking dish. Shape into a loaf. **Topping:** Lay bacon strips on top of meat loaf. Mix ingredients for topping and spread on loaf. Bake for 1 hour.

PINEAPPLE CHICKEN
Lilly Moore

6 chicken wings or legs or boneless
  breasts, cut in pieces
¾ c. brown sugar
¾ c. wine vinegar
¾ c. barbecue sauce

Chopped onions (opt.)
½ c. bell pepper (opt.)
2 T. cornstarch
½ c. chunk pineapple
½ c. celery (opt.)

Mix first 7 ingredients. Pour over chicken.

SHELLY ROBISON'S TUNA NOODLE CASSEROLE

12-oz. bag extra-wide egg noodles
1 (5-oz.) can tuna in oil, drained
2 (10-oz.) cans cream of mushroom

½ (9-oz.) bag Lays potato chips,
  crushed
2 c. shredded cheddar cheese

Cook noodles until tender and drain. Add tuna and cream of mushroom. Mix well, then add chips. Pour into casserole dish. Sprinkle cheese on top. Place in preheated 400° oven until heated through and cheese is golden brown.

TAMALE PIE
Louise Cowell

1 lb. lean ground beef
1 can whole kernel corn
2 cans tomato sauce
1 ½ tsp. salt
½ c. corn meal

1 sm. onion
1 can olives
1 c. shredded cheese
2 T. chili powder
1 ½ c. milk

Cook ground beef and 1 teaspoon salt until lightly browned, crumble size. Add chopped onion and cook until slightly tender. Add chili powder and stir. Add whole kernel corn and tomato sauce to the mixture and set aside. In a small saucepan, combine corn meal, ½ teaspoon salt and milk. Cook over medium heat until lightly thickened. Remove from heat and add to the ground beef mixture, stirring slightly, adding a can of pitted olives. Pour mixture into a 9 x 12-inch baking dish. Bake at 350° for about 30 minutes. Sprinkle shredded cheese over top and bake about 5 more minutes, or until cheese has melted.

GREEN ENCHILADAS

Kelly Edwards

2 chicken breasts, boiled in water
   with fresh garlic until done, 6 to
   8 minutes
1 can Ortega green chili enchilada
   sauce
1 ½ c. shredded Monterey Jack
   cheese

1 ½ c. shredded Cheddar cheese
1 c. chopped onion
1 pkg. flour tortillas
Sour cream

Shred boiled chicken and set aside. In a 9 x 13-inch pan, put small layer of enchilada sauce. With flour tortilla laying flat, put equal amounts of chicken and cheese. Add onion to taste. Roll up and place in pan. Repeat until pan is full. Pour remaining sauce over and cover with remaining cheese. Bake at 350° for 25 minutes. Top with sour cream and serve with Spanish rice and salad.

BROCCOLI & RICE CASSEROLE

Robin Marshall

2 pkgs. Success Rice
½ cube of butter
1 lg. jar Cheez Whiz

1 can cream of chicken soup
2 pkgs. frozen chopped broccoli
1 can stems and pieces, mushrooms

Cook broccoli and rice. Add in the rest of the ingredients and mix well. Pour in baking dish and bake on 350° for 30 minutes. **Tip:** May add chicken and serve as a main dish.

SPECIAL POT ROAST

M. Smith

2 T. vegetable oil
1 can cream of mushroom soup
1 can French onion soup or 1 env.
   dry onion soup mix plus 1 can
   water

2- to 4-lb. chuck/pot roast

Brown roast in Dutch oven with vegetable oil. Mix soup in bowl. After roast is browned, drain oil. Pour soup over roast. Seal with aluminum foil. Cook in 325° oven for at least 3 hours. If you want to use a crockpot, place meat in crockpot. Pour soups over roast. Cook on high for 4 to 6 hours, low for 6 to 8 hours.

CORNISH GAME HENS

John Pierce

4 Cornish game hens, thawed
½ c. melted butter

½ tsp. minced garlic
½ tsp. each: salt and pepper

Place hens in large bowl. Combine garlic, butter, salt and pepper into mixture. Coat with brush over hens and let marinate for 1 hour in refrigerator. Take hens and place in large covered casserole dish, then coat again on all sides with mixture. Coat about every 20 minutes while baking. Bake, uncovered, at 350° for 4 hours. Place hens on serving platter. Surround hens with wild rice and drizzle a little mixture over hens and rice.

126207-15

CHICKEN ENCHILADA

Kelly Edwards

1 c. Cheddar cheese
1 c. Monterey Jack cheese
1 (8-oz.) ctn. sour cream
1 can cream of chicken soup
1 sm. can green chilies, diced
4 flour tortillas
3 boneless chicken breasts

Boil chicken breasts for about 30 minutes and cut up into cubes. Shred both Monterey and Cheddar cheese. Mix sour cream, cream soup, chilies and chicken in large bowl. Lay 2 tortillas in bottom of casserole dish. Cover tortillas with ½ of sauce mixture. Sprinkle with ½ of cheese mixture on top of sauce. Repeat with tortillas, sauce mixture and cheeses. Top with any remaining cheese. Bake at 350° for 30 minutes, uncovered.

CHICKEN PINEAPPLE CHEESE SUPREME

Kelly Edwards

1 (9-oz.) pkg. Green Giant Harvest
  Fresh frozen broccoli spears
4 boneless, skinless chicken breast
  halves
3 T. flour
½ tsp. salt
⅛ tsp. white pepper
2 tsp. margarine or butter
1 (8-oz.) can pineapple sliced,
  drained
4 oz. Monterey Jack cheese

Cook broccoli as directed on package. Place 1 chicken breast half, bones side up, between 2 pieces of plastic wrap or waxed paper. Working from the center, beat chicken. Repeat with remaining chicken breasts. In shallow pan, combine flour, salt and pepper. Coat chicken with flour mixture. Melt margarine or butter in large skillet. Add chicken and cook 5 to 6 minutes on each side, or until chicken is fork-tender and juices run clear. Place pineapple slice on each chicken breast. Drain broccoli, top each pineapple slice with ¼ of broccoli spears and 1 slice of cheese. Repeat for all 4 chicken breasts. Cover and cook an additional minutes or until cheese is melted.

LAWRY'S MEXICAN LASAGNE

Kelly Edwards

1 ½ lbs. ground beef
1 tsp. seasoned salt
1 (1 ¼-oz.) pkg. taco seasoning mix
1 c. diced tomatoes, fresh or
  canned
2 (8-oz.) cans tomato sauce
1 (4-oz.) can diced green chilies
8 oz. ricotta cheese
2 eggs
9 tortillas
10 oz. Monterey Jack cheese,
  shredded

Brown beef in a large skillet until crumbly. Drain. Add seasoned salt, taco seasoning, tomatoes, tomato sauce and chilies. Blend well and bring to a boil. Reduce heat and simmer, uncovered, 10 minutes. In a small bowl, combine ricotta cheese and eggs. In the bottom of a 9 x 13-inch baking dish, spread half of the meat mixture. Top with half of the tortillas. Spread with half of the ricotta cheese mixture over the tortillas and top with half of the Jack cheese. Repeat once more, ending with the grated cheese. Bake, uncovered, at 350° for 20 to 30 minutes. Let stand 10 minutes before cutting. Makes 8 servings.

IMPOSSIBLE CHEESEBURGER PIE

Kelly Edwards

1 lb. ground beef
1 c. chopped onions
½ tsp. salt
1 c. shredded cheese

1 c. milk
½ c. Bisquick baking mix
2 eggs

Cook ground beef and onion and drain. Stir in salt. Spread in greased 9-inch pie plate. Sprinkle with cheese. Stir remaining ingredients with fork until blended. Pour into plate. Bake at 400° for 25 minutes, or until knife comes out clean. Serves 8.

CHICKEN TETRAZZINI

Kelly Edwards

1 ½ lbs. chicken breasts
Bell pepper
Onion
Celery
1 sm. jar pimentos
1 can cream of chicken soup

1 lb. Velveeta cheese, cubed
Salt
Pepper
½ to ¾ pkg. spaghetti or thin
  vermicelli
Chicken broth, reserved

Boil chicken with bell pepper, onion and celery. Cut chicken into small pieces. Cook spaghetti in chicken broth. Drain. Mix spaghetti with chicken, pimento, mushrooms, Ro-Tel tomatoes, diced tomatoes, soup, cheese, salt, pepper and 1 cup of broth. Mix well. Place in large baking dish. Bake at 350° to 400° for 30 minutes, until cheese melts and mixture is slightly brown. This will feed many people.

CHICKEN DIVAN

Lilly

1 lg. bag frozen broccoli
5 to 6 boneless chicken breasts
2 cans cream of chicken soup
1 c. mayonnaise
2 tsp. lemon juice

½ tsp. curry powder
1 c. shredded sharp cheddar cheese
½ box seasoned bread crumbs
1 T. melted butter

Preheat oven to 350°. Steam or pre-bake chicken. Cook broccoli. Put broccoli in 9 x 12-inch dish. Spread chicken over broccoli. Combine in mixing bowl all other ingredients except butter and bread crumbs. Mix well. Spread over top of chicken. Sprinkle bread crumbs on top. Pour butter lightly around edge. Bake 35 to 45 minutes.

SAUSAGE BALLS

Janice Pelham

1 (1-lb.) pkg. ground sausage
3 c. baking mix (recommended:
  Bisquick)

4 c. grated sharp Cheddar
⅛ tsp. pepper

Dip:

1 c. mayonnaise

1 T. mustard

Preheat the oven to 375°. Spray a baking sheet with vegetable oil cooking spray. Combine all ingredients in a large glass bowl. Mix well with your fingers. The mixture will be very crumbly. Form into 1-inch balls, squeezing the mixture so it holds

(continued)

126207-15

together, then rolling it between the palms of your hands to form balls. Place the balls on the baking sheet. Bake for 18 to 20 minutes, or until golden brown. To prevent sticking, move the balls with a spatula halfway through cooking. To make the dip, combine the mayonnaise and mustard. Serve with sausage balls. **Tip:** These are perfect to take along to a pot luck or brunch! You can spice these up with jalapeños or chizo. Another Paula Deen favorite!

CREAMED CHICKEN & BISCUITS

Lilly, Suzzie & Cherrie Moore

½ lg. onion
1 ½ tsp. butter
4 c. chopped cooked chicken
1 (10¾-oz.) can cream of chicken
   soup

1 c. sour cream
½ c. milk
1 c. shredded mild cheddar cheese,
   divided
6 frozen biscuits, thawed

Preheat oven to 350°. Grease the bottom and sides of an 11 x 7-inch baking dish. Chop the onion. Heat butter in a small nonstick skillet over medium-high heat until melted. Stir in onion. Sauté until tender. Combine onion, chicken, soup, sour cream and milk in a medium bowl and mix well. Spoon mixture into prepared baking dish. Bake for 15 minutes. Remove from oven. Sprinkle baked layer with ¾ cup of the Cheddar. Arrange biscuits in single layer over top. Sprinkle with remaining Cheddar. Bake until biscuits are golden brown and the sauce is bubbly, about 20 minutes longer. Serve immediately.

MEAT LOAF

Lucy Bowen

2 lbs. hamburger
1 sm. onion, chopped*
12 crackers, crushed(**)
3 eggs

1 tsp. salt
½ tsp. pepper
1 T. Italian seasoning

Mix well and bake at 350° until done. Serve with brown gravy and scalloped potatoes. Can top with meat loaf with tomato sauce if desired. *Onion soup mix. (**)Cracker meal, ½.

GRANDMA BOWEN'S ITALIAN SPAGHETTI (1959)

Lucy Bowen

4 slices bacon, chopped
1 lb. lean hamburger
1 ½ c. celery, chopped
1 onion, chopped
1 sm. can mushrooms, sliced
1 c. black olives, sliced, or 1 c.
   green stuffed olives, sliced

1 tsp. salt
1 tsp. pepper
1 T. Italian seasoning
2 cans tomatoes
2 cans tomato paste

Brown hamburger and bacon. Add rest of ingredients and simmer 2 hours. Cook and drain spaghetti. Put spaghetti on plate and cover with sauce.

MAY ROBISON'S GOULASH

4 c. water
2 lbs. ground beef
1 (15-oz.) can tomato sauce
2 (15-oz.) cans Italian tomatoes

1 can whole kernel corn, drained
2 c. elbow noodles
Salt and pepper to taste

Place all ingredients in either a slow cooker or pot. Bring to a boil, then simmer until hamburger meat is cooked and elbow noodles are tender.

ELIZABETH ROBISON'S CHIX ALFREDO PASTA

3 chicken breasts, seasoned and cooked, then shredded
1-lb. box bow tie noodles, cooked and drained

3 (16-oz.) jars Ragu Alfredo roasted garlic Parmesan sauce

Mix all ingredients and heat thoroughly over low heat. Serve with grated Parmesan cheese and garlic toast. **Additions:** Steamed broccoli, sliced mushrooms cooked in butter.

FRIED HOMEMADE CHICKEN STRIPS

Rhonda Pierce

2 to 3 c. flour
5 eggs
Salt and pepper
1 to 2 c. vegetable oil
½ to 1 c. plain corn flakes or saltine crackers

2 lbs. fresh chicken tender strips or chicken breasts, cut into sm. strips

Crack all eggs and put into a medium-size mixing bowl or pie plate. Blend eggs like making scrambled eggs, then salt and pepper. Smash up corn flakes and mix with flour, salt and pepper, then put into pie plate or dish. Get large frying pan or skillet, put oil in frying pan up to ½ inch deep and put over medium fire. Let frying pan get hot while getting strips ready. Wash chicken. Cut into strips or purchase fresh chicken strips already cut. Drop into egg batter and then into flour mixture. Turn over strips, coating all areas of each chicken strip. When you get a few pieces done, drop them into frying pan to start cooking. Turn every so often until golden brown, then put on plate or pan with a paper towel under to catch oil, so chicken isn't greasy and after a few minutes, serve.

TOPPING FOR HAM

Betty Gallagher

1 c. light brown sugar
1 T. prepared mustard

1 T. vinegar

Put on 15 minutes before ham is done. Put on top and sides of ham.

44

126207-15

BEEF KABASA

6 pkgs. Kabasa meat
¾ c. cilantro
1 red onion, chopped
Mustard
Honey

4 bell peppers
¾ c. jalapeño
3 (20-oz.) bottles BBQ sauce
Fresh ground pepper

Put all on stove in pan and cook together.

CHICAGO-STYLE PIZZA

1 (1-lb.) loaf frozen bread dough,
   thawed
1 lb. bulk Italian sausage
2 c. shredded mozzarella cheese
2 tsp. olive oil
8 oz. sliced fresh mushrooms
1 sm. onion, chopped
1 (28-oz.) can diced tomatoes,
   drained

¾ tsp. dried oregano
½ tsp. salt
¼ tsp. fennel seed
¼ tsp. garlic powder
½ c. freshly grated Parmesan
   cheese

Preheat oven to 350°. Press dough into the bottom and up the sides of a greased 9 x 13-inch baking dish. (You'll need to gently stretch the dough as you press it into the pan.) Crumble sausage into a large skillet over medium-high heat. Cook and stir until evenly browned. Remove sausage with a slotted spoon and sprinkle over dough crust. Sprinkle mozzarella evenly. Heat oil in skillet. Add mushrooms and onion and cook and stir until onion is tender. Stir in tomatoes, oregano, salt, fennel seed and garlic powder. Spoon over mozzarella. Sprinkle Parmesan over the top. Bake for 25 to 35 minutes in preheated oven or until crust is golden brown. (May take 45 minutes for the crust to brown.)

HOMEMADE NOODLES

Lucy Bowen

6 egg yolks, separated
3 c. flour

6 T. water
½ tsp. salt

Beat the egg yolks and water together thoroughly. Stir in salt and flour to make a very stiff yet workable dough. Divide the dough into 4 small balls. Roll each one out, very thin. Let each on a dry cloth to dry. When dry enough not to stick together, cut into thin strips. Allow noodles to completely dry before storing in an airtight container.

SWISS STEAK

Sharon's Grandma

1 round steak, tenderized
1 onion, chopped
Salt, pepper and garlic to taste
1 can tomato soup

1 can cream of mushroom soup
1 c. flour
¼ c. oil
½ can of water

Cut steak into serving size, about 3 x 4-inch piece. Then add flour, salt, pepper and garlic into a Baggie and mix. Put oil into a skillet and heat, making sure skillet

(continued)

is hot. Add steak to flour mixture and coat, then put into skillet and brown on both sides. Take meat out of skillet and put into a 9 x 13-inch baking dish. Set aside. In same skillet, add onion and cook about 3 minutes, then add soups and water. Cook until hot. Pour over meat. Put in 350° oven for 1½ hours or until tender.

SLIPPERY DUMPLINGS
Betty Montgomery

2 c. flour
2 tsp. baking powder
½ tsp. salt

3 T. shortening
½ to ¾ c. hot water

Combine flour, baking powder and salt; mix. Cut in shortening. Add hot water, a little at a time, until dough is firm. Roll out dough to ¹⁄₁₆-inch thickness and cut into 2-inch squares. Drop into broth. Add 1 tablespoon butter to broth. Always remove chicken from broth while dumplings cook slowly, about 30 minutes. Cut chicken into bite-size pieces and add last.

CROCKPOT ROUND STEAK
Betty Montgomery

2 lbs. round steak, cut into serving-
   size pieces

½ pkg. onion soup mix
10¾ oz. mushroom soup

Place meat into slow cooker. Salt and pepper to taste. Add onion soup and mushroom soup. Last add ¼ cup water. Cook on low heat 6 to 8 hours.

BEEF & BISCUIT BAKE
Edna Welch

1 lb. ground beef
1 (16-oz.) can kidney beans
1 (15¼-oz.) can kernel corn,
   drained
1 (10¾-oz.) can condensed tomato
   soup, undiluted
¼ c. milk
2 T. minced onion

½ tsp. chili powder
¼ tsp. salt
1 c. cubed process American cheese
1 (12-oz.) tube refrigerated biscuits
2 to 3 T. butter or margarine,
   melted
⅓ c. yellow corn meal

In a saucepan, over medium heat, brown beef; drain. Add beans, corn, soup, milk, onions, chili powder and salt. Bring to a boil. Remove from heat; stir in cheese until melted. Spoon into a greased 2½-quart baking dish. Bake, uncovered, at 375° for 10 minutes. Meanwhile, brush all sides of biscuits with butter. Roll in corn meal. Place on top of bubbling meat mixture. Return to oven for 10 to 12 minutes, or until biscuits are lightly browned and cooked through. Makes 6 to 8 servings.

46

Breads & Rolls

Helpful Hints

- When baking bread, a small dish of water in the oven will keep the crust from getting too hard or brown.

- Use shortening, not margarine or oil, to grease pans when baking bread. Margarine and oil absorb more readily into the dough.

- To make self-rising flour, mix 4 cups flour, 2 teaspoons salt, and 2 tablespoons baking powder. Store in a tightly covered container.

- One scant tablespoon of bulk yeast is equal to one packet of yeast.

- Hot water kills yeast. One way to test for the correct temperature is to pour the water over your wrist. If you cannot feel hot or cold, the temperature is just right.

- When in doubt, always sift flour before measuring.

- Use bread flour for baking heavier breads, such as mixed grain, pizza doughs, bagels, etc.

- When baking in a glass pan, reduce the oven temperature by 25°.

- When baking bread, you can achieve a finer texture if you use milk. Water makes a coarser bread.

- Fill an empty salt shaker with flour to quickly and easily dust a bread pan or work surface.

- For successful quick breads, do not overmix the dough. Mix only until combined. An overmixed batter creates tough and rubbery muffins, biscuits, and quick breads.

- Muffins can be eaten warm. Most other quick breads taste better the next day. Nut breads are better if stored 24 hours before serving.

- Nuts, shelled or unshelled, keep best and longest when stored in the freezer. Unshelled nuts crack more easily when frozen. Nuts can be used directly from the freezer.

- Enhance the flavor of nuts, such as almonds, walnuts, and pecans, by toasting them before using in recipes. Place nuts on a baking sheet and bake at 300° for 5−8 minutes or until slightly browned.

- Overripe bananas can be frozen until it's time to bake. Store them unpeeled in a plastic bag.

- The freshness of eggs can be tested by placing them in a large bowl of cold water; if they float, do not use them.

BREADS & ROLLS

CINNAMON ROLLS
(Use Sweet Roll Recipe)

Roll out bread dough thin as possible, ¼ inch. Smear oleo over rolled out dough. Sprinkle cinnamon and brown sugar. Add chopped walnuts and/or raisins. Roll dough by hand into roll; seal seams. Cut into ½- to 1-inch slices. Put in pan. Let rise. Bake at 350° until golden brown.

SWEET ROLL RECIPE
(1957)

Lucy Bowen

8 c. flour
1 c. milk
1 ½ c. water
1 to 2 yeast cakes

½ c. sugar
4 tsp. salt
2 eggs
¼ c. shortening

Scald milk and melt shortening. Add salt and sugar to milk mixture. **Let cool!** Add yeast. Add beaten eggs and water. Add ½ of the flour and mix well. Add rest of flour and work dough until flour is gone. Let rise 2 hours. Knead down and make rolls/loaves of bread. Let rise and bake at 400°.

MOTHER'S CORNBREAD

Edna Welch

1 egg
⅓ c. flour
¾ c. cornmeal
½ tsp. baking powder

½ tsp. baking soda
Salt to taste
Buttermilk to mix

Mix dry ingredients. Add buttermilk. Pour into greased cast-iron skillet. Bake at 500° until lightly browned.

MOTHER'S BUTTERMILK BISCUITS

Edna Welch

1 c. flour
½ tsp. baking soda
½ tsp. baking powder

Salt
1 heaping spoonful shortening
Just enough buttermilk to moisten

Mix dry ingredients. Mix in shortening. Add buttermilk. Knead and pinch off section. Place in greased cast-iron skillet. Bake at 500° until lightly browned.

HONEY-WHEAT BATTER BREAD
(No Cholesterol)

Lucy Bowen

1 pkg. active dry yeast
1 ¼ c. warm water (105° to 115°)
1 c. all-purpose flour
1 c. whole wheat flour
2 T. wheat germ

2 T. honey
2 T. shortening
2 tsp. salt
1 c. whole wheat flour

(continued)

Dissolve yeast in warm water in a large bowl. Add all ingredients except 1 cup whole wheat flour. Beat on low speed until moistened. Beat on medium speed 2 minutes, scraping bowl occasionally. Stir in remaining 1 cup whole wheat flour 1 minute to 1 minute and 30 seconds, or until smooth. Scrape batter from side of bowl. Cover and let rise in warm place about 45 minutes, or until double.

FLUFFY BISCUIT MUFFINS

Edna Welch

1 c. self-rising flour
2 T. mayonnaise (no substitutes)

½ c. milk

In a bowl, cut flour and mayonnaise together until mixture resembles coarse crumbs. Add milk. Stir just until mixed. Spoon into 4 greased muffin cups. Bake at 425° for 14 to 16 minutes, or until lightly browned. Yields 4 biscuits.

MONKEY BREAD

Joyce Goodwin

4 cans biscuits, cut into fourths
½ tsp. cinnamon

⅔ c. sugar

Topping:

1 tsp. cinnamon
1 ½ sticks oleo

1 c. brown sugar

Cut biscuits and roll each piece in cinnamon and sugar. Grease bundt pan and line bottom with chopped nuts. Place layer of biscuit pieces, then nuts, etc. Pour topping over top and bake at 350° for 20 to 25 minutes. Test with fork in center. Let cool 10 minutes before removing from pan. **Topping:** Melt butter and mix with cinnamon and sugar.

BUTTERMILK BISCUITS

Tom Edgar

2 c. all-purpose flour
1 T. baking powder
¾ tsp. salt
½ tsp. baking soda

5 tsp. chilled solid vegetable
    shortening
1 c. buttermilk

Preheat the oven to 425°. In a large bowl, sift together flour, baking powder, salt and baking soda. Using a pastry blender or 2 knives, cut the shortening into the flour mixture until coarse crumbs form. Add the buttermilk, tossing with a fork until a dough forms. Turn dough out onto a lightly floured surface. Gather into a disk. Knead lightly a few times just until smooth. The dough can be made up to 2 hours ahead, wrapped until ready to use. Pat the dough to ¾ inch thick. Using a biscuit cutter or a glass dipped in flour, cut out biscuits. Place the biscuits 2 inches apart on an ungreased baking sheet. Bake.

126207-15

JALAPEÑO CORN BREAD

Betty Montgomery

1 c. yellow cornmeal
½ c. flour
1 tsp. salt
½ tsp. baking soda
1 sm. can cream corn
¼ med. onion, diced

2 T. jalapeño, diced
⅓ c. Cheddar, grated
¼ c. oil
2 eggs, slightly beaten
1 c. buttermilk

Grease an 8-inch skillet. Heat to very hot. Batter should sizzle when poured into pan. Bake at 425° for 30 minutes, or until nice and brown.

ZUCCHINI BREAD

Linda Hogan

3 c. flour
1 tsp. baking soda
½ tsp. baking powder
1 tsp. salt
3 tsp. cinnamon
1 tsp. allspice
½ tsp. nutmeg

2 ⅔ c. sugar
1 c. oil
2 eggs
2 tsp. vanilla
2 c. zucchini, diced
1 (8-oz.) can crushed pineapple

Cream sugar, oil, crushed pineapple, vanilla, zucchini and eggs. Fold in dry ingredients. Stir well. Bake in loaf pans at 350° for 1 hour, or until done.

PEPPER CHEESE BREAD

1 tsp. Quaker or Aunt Jemima
   enriched corn meal
2 to 2 ½ c. all-purpose flour
1 c. Quaker Oat Bran hot cereal,
   uncooked
2 tsp. sugar
½ to 1 tsp. pepper

1 pkg. quick-rise yeast
⅛ tsp. baking soda
1 c. water
¼ c. skim milk
2 T. margarine
1 c. (4 oz.) shredded low fat
   cheddar cheese

Lightly spray 8 x 4-inch loaf pan with vegetable oil cooking spray or oil lightly. Sprinkle sides and bottom with corn meal. In a large mixer bowl, combine 1 cup flour, oat bran, sugar, pepper, yeast and baking soda. Heat water, milk and margarine until very warm (120° to 130°). Add to dry ingredients; beat at low speed of electric mixer until moistened. Add cheese. Increase speed to medium. Continue beating 3 minutes. Stir in enough remaining flour to form a stiff dough. Turn out onto lightly floured surface. Knead 8 to 10 minutes, or until dough is smooth and elastic. Roll into 15 x 7-inch rectangle. Starting at narrow end, roll up dough tightly. Pinch ends and seam to seal; place seam side down in prepared pan. Cover; let rise in warm place about 30 minutes, or until doubled in size. Heat oven to 375°. Bake 30 to 35 minutes, or until golden brown. Remove from pan; cool on wire rack at least 1 hour before slicing. Serve as sandwich bread or as a main meal accompaniment. Makes 16 slices.

PEANUT BUTTER PUMPKIN BREAD

3 c. sugar or ½ c. Baking Splenda
1 (15-oz.) can solid pack pumpkin
1 c. vegetable or canola oil
3 ½ c. all-purpose flour
1 ½ tsp. salt
1 tsp. ground nutmeg

4 eggs
¾ c. water
⅔ c. peanut butter
2 tsp. baking soda
1 tsp. ground cinnamon

In a mixing bowl, combine the sugar, pumpkin, eggs, oil, water and peanut butter; beat well. Combine the flour, baking soda, salt, cinnamon and nutmeg. Gradually add to pumpkin mixture; mix well. Pour into 2 greased 9 x 5 x 3-inch loaf pans. Bake at 350° for 60 to 70 minutes, or until a toothpick comes out clean. Cool for 10 minutes before removing from pans to wire racks. Makes 2 loaves.

COUNTRY CORNBREAD DRESSING   Louise Cowell

9 x 13-inch cornbread
1 can chicken broth
1 tsp. salt
¼ tsp. black pepper

¼ c. chopped onions
¼ c. chopped celery
1 tsp. sage
1 tsp. poultry seasoning

Cook cornbread a day before so it it's cold. Combine celery and onions with half water and half chicken broth. Once mixture is hot, add a little butter and salt in saucepan until tender (just simmer), not much liquid left in pan. Crumble cornbread in bowl. Add sage and poultry seasoning. Add chicken broth, veggie mixture and black pepper. Add ¼ cup of turkey broth at a time, until is has a texture like oatmeal. Taste it to see if it is okay. Put in oiled 9 x 13-inch pan, then put in oven for 30 minutes around 350° for softer taste or 375° for crunchier taste.

COUNTRY CORNBREAD   Louise Cowell

2 c. yellow corn meal
½ tsp. baking soda
1 c. flour
1 ¼ tsp. salt

2 ½ tsp. baking powder
1 ½ c. milk or more
2 eggs
½ c. butter or ¼ c. shortening or oil

Mix all dry ingredients together. Add milk to dry ingredients and mix thoroughly. Add eggs and beat well. Mix in softened butter or shortening or oil. If batter it too thick, add more milk until you get a cake-like batter. Pour into a well greased 9 x 13-inch pan or similar. Bake at 350° for 30 minutes. Top should be brown.

QUICKY STICKY BUNS   Rhonda Pierce
(Pecan Rolls)

½ c. packed brown sugar
½ c. butter or margarine, softened
2 (8-oz.) tubes refrigerated crescent
  rolls

1 tsp. ground cinnamon
¼ c. corn syrup
⅔ c. chopped pecans
¼ c. sugar

In a small bowl, combine brown sugar, butter and corn syrup. Spread in 2 greased 8-inch square baking pan; set aside. Unroll each tube of crescent roll dough into

(continued)

a rectangle. Seal seams and perforations. Combine pecans, sugar and cinnamon. Sprinkle over dough. Roll up, jelly roll style, starting with a long side. Seal edge. Cut each roll into 16 slices. Place, cut side down, in prepared pans. Bake at 375° for 13 to 17 minutes, or until golden brown. Cool in pans for 1 minute before inverting onto serving plates. Makes 32 rolls.

GOLDEN CARROT MUFFINS
Dolly Barton

¼ c. butter
½ c. sour cream
4 oz. crushed pineapple
4 oz. fresh grated carrots
1 egg
1 c. sugar

¼ c. cocoa
1 tsp. baking powder
¼ tsp. soda
¼ tsp. salt
¼ c. chopped walnuts
1 c. flour

Mix all ingredients together and pour into 12-cup muffin pan. Heat oven to 350°.

Icing:

1 (8-oz.) box cream cheese

1 jar marshmallow creme

Beat together and put on cool cakes.

ZUCCHINI NUT BREAD
Dolly Barton

2 eggs
1 c. oil
2 c. grated zucchini
2 c. sugar
2 tsp. vanilla

3 c. flour
1 tsp. baking soda
½ tsp. baking powder
1 tsp. salt
3 tsp. cinnamon

In separate bowl, sift together dry ingredients. Beat eggs until foamy, then add next 4 ingredients. Do not use beater. Mix well after each ingredients. Add 1 cup nuts; divide into 2 loaves, greased and floured pans. Bake at 350° for 1 hour.

CARROT BREAD
Dolly Barton

⅓ c. Crisco shortening
2 eggs
1 tsp. baking powder
½ tsp. salt
½ c. crushed pineapple

½ c. sugar
1 ¾ c. flour
½ tsp. soda
½ c. carrots, shredded
½ c. walnuts

Mix all ingredients with electric mixer. Pour into well greased loaf pan. Heat oven to 350°. Bake 50 minutes, or until done. Wrap and store overnight.

ROBIN'S BROWNIES
Robin Marshall

¾ c. all-purpose flour
½ c. butter
2 eggs, beaten
¼ c. cocoa

¼ tsp. salt
1 c. sugar
1 tsp. vanilla
¾ c. chopped nuts

(continued)

Mix all ingredients together. Place into buttered brownie pan. Bake for 20 minutes at 350°.

ALICIES' BREAD PUDDING

½ loaf French bread, cubed
5 whole eggs
1 qt. milk
1 tsp. vanilla
½ c. raisins
2 c. sugar
½ tsp. cinnamon
1 c. butter

Mix together eggs, milk and vanilla. Then in separate bowl, mix sugar and cinnamon. Spray pan with Pam. Put ½ cup raisins and bread cubes into baking dish. Pour liquid mixture over it. Melt 1 cup butter and pour ½ of it over mixture and marble it around. Pour sugar and cinnamon over all. Add remaining half of the butter on top of sugar. Bake at 350° in water pan until done. Stick knife in. If it comes out clean, about 1¼ hours, it's done.

CHOCOLATE CHIP BREAD PUDDING

1 loaf cinnamon raisin bread, cut into cubes
1 c. mini semisweet chocolate chips
3 c. chocolate milk
¼ c. packed dark brown sugar
1 T. confectioners' sugar
4 lg. eggs
1 tsp. vanilla extract

Preheat oven to 350°. Coat a 9 x 2-inch square baking pan with nonstick cooking spray. In a large bowl, toss bread with ¾ cup of the mini chips. In a medium bowl, whisk together chocolate milk, eggs, brown sugar and vanilla. Pour mixture into bread machine, then transfer to prepared baking pan, pressing down lightly. Sprinkle with remaining ¼ cup mini chips. Bake at 350° for 45 minutes. Dust with confectioners' sugar just before serving.

BLUEBERRY ZUCCHINI BREAD   *Janice McWhorter*

3 eggs
1 c. vegetable oil
3 tsp. vanilla
2¼ c. white sugar
2 c. shredded zucchini
3 c. all-purpose flour
1 tsp. salt
1 tsp. baking powder
¼ tsp. baking soda
1 T. cinnamon
1 pt. fresh or frozen blueberries

Preheat oven to 350°. Lightly grease 4 mini loaf pans. In a large bowl, beat together eggs, oil, vanilla and sugar. Fold in zucchini. Beat in flour, salt, baking powder, baking soda and cinnamon. Gently fold in blueberries. Pour into pans. Bake 50 minutes, or until knife inserted into loaf comes out clean. Cool 20 minutes. Turn onto wire racks to cool completely.

126207-15

BANANA BREAD
Christal Montgomery

3 lg. very ripe bananas
1 egg
1 ½ c. flour
¾ tsp. soda

1 c. sugar
½ c. butter, melted
¾ tsp. salt

Mash bananas with fork. Blend in sugar, egg and butter. Add flour, salt and soda; mix well. Pour batter into greased and floured 9 x 5 x 3-inch loaf pan. Bake at 325° for approximately 1 hour. Makes 1 loaf. **Optional:** ½ cup nuts.

BISQUICK BANANA NUT BREAD
Lucy Bowen

1 ⅓ c. mashed bananas
⅔ c. sugar
¼ c. milk
3 T. vegetable oil

½ tsp. vanilla
3 eggs
2 ⅔ c. Bisquick mix
½ c. chopped nuts

Heat oven to 350°. Grease bottom of 9 x 5 x 3-inch loaf pan. Stir in bananas, sugar, milk, oil, vanilla and eggs in a large bowl. Stir in Bisquick mix and nuts. Bake 50 to 60 minutes, or until toothpick inserted in center comes out clean. Cool 15 minutes. Loosen sides of loaf pan; remove and place, top side up, on a wire rack. Cool completely (2 hours) before slicing. Wrap tightly and store at room temperature up to 4 days or refrigerate up to 10 days.

BROCCOLI CORNBREAD

2 pkgs. Jiffy corn muffin mix
5 eggs
1 (16 oz.) cottage cheese or 2 c.
1 (14-oz.) pkg. frozen chopped
  broccoli, thawed

1 ½ sticks melted butter
1 med. onion, chopped
½ c. shredded cheddar cheese

in a large bowl, mix together eggs and cottage cheese. Mix well. Add muffin mix last. Mix well and pour into a 9 x 13-inch greased pan. Bake at 375° for 45 to 60 minutes, until golden brown and toothpick inserted in center comes out clean. Enjoy. (I use a larger pan so it won't be so thick.)

PARKER HOUSE ROLLS
Lucy Bowen

8 c. flour
1 c. milk
1 ½ c. water
1 to 2 yeast cakes

½ c. sugar
4 tsp. salt
2 eggs
¼ c. shortening

Scald milk and shortening and add salt and sugar. Mix well. Add yeast and 3 cups of flour and mix well. Let rise 1 hour. Add rest of flour and work dough until flour is gone. Let rise 1 ½ hours. Knead down and make rolls and let rise, then bake. I use this recipe for cinnamon rolls. Bake at 400°.

BUTTERMILK BISCUITS

Barbara Hosman

2 ½ c. self-rising flour
2 tsp. sugar
½ c. butter or shortening

¾ to 1 c. buttermilk, milk or
whipping cream

Stir together flour and sugar. Use pastry blender or fork, cut in butter until it is crumbly. Stir in buttermilk until dough leaves side of bowl. If dough is dry, stir in 1 to 2 teaspoons additional buttermilk. On lightly floured surface, knead dough just until smooth. Roll to ½-inch thickness. Cut dough with cutter; roll in a ball. On ungreased cookie sheet 1 inch apart, bake at 450° for 10 to 12 minutes. Serves 12.

ZUCCHINI BREAD

Lilly

⅓ c. shortening
½ c. sugar
2 eggs
1 ½ c. flour (self-rising, don't put in
baking powder and baking soda)

1 tsp. baking powder
½ tsp. baking soda
½ tsp. salt
1 c. grated zucchini
½ c. pecans or walnuts

Mix shortening, sugar and eggs first, then all other ingredients. Use a 9 x 5-inch or 2 (6 x 4-inch) pans. Bake 45 minutes at 350° or until well done.

ZUCCHINI MUFFINS

Robin Marshall

3 c. flour
1 tsp. baking soda
½ tsp. baking powder
1 tsp. cinnamon
1 tsp. allspice
½ tsp. nutmeg
2 ⅔ c. sugar

1 c. oil
2 eggs
2 tsp. vanilla
2 c. grated zucchini (cheese grater
works well)
1 (8 oz.) crushed pineapple

Mix all liquid together, then add all dry. Makes 24 muffins. (Instead of cinnamon, allspice and nutmeg, use 4 tablespoons of pumpkin pie spice.) Bake at 350° until golden brown.

PUMPKIN BREAD

Betty Montgomery

2 c. sugar
4 eggs
1 tsp. cinnamon
3 ½ c. flour
2 c. pumpkin
2 greased and floured pans

1 c. oil
1 ½ tsp. salt
1 tsp. nutmeg
2 tsp. soda
⅔ c. water

Preheat oven to 350°. Mix sugar, oil, eggs and 2 cups pumpkin. Add salt, cinnamon and nutmeg. Mix flour and soda separately. Add to other ingredients and mix. Bake for 1 hour. Makes 2 loaves.

126207-15

CRANBERRY-WALNUT MUFFINS

Nonstick cooking spray
1 c. all-purpose flour
½ c. white whole wheat flour
¼ c. quick-cooking rolled oats
2 tsp. baking powder
½ tsp. ground cinnamon or apple
    pie spice
¼ tsp. salt

1 egg, lightly beaten
¾ c. fat-free milk
½ c. sugar
3 T. canola oil
⅓ c. dried cranberries, coarsely
    chopped
¼ c. walnuts, toasted and chopped

Preheat oven to 375°. Coat 12 (2½-inch) muffin cups with cooking spray or line with paper baking cups; set aside. In a large bowl, combine all-purpose and whole wheat flours, oats, baking powder, cinnamon and salt. In medium bowl, combine egg, milk, sugar and oil. Add egg mixture, all at once, to flour mixture. Stir just until combined. Fold in cranberries and walnuts. Spoon batter into prepared cups. Bake 15 to 18 minutes, or until tops are lightly browned and toothpick inserted in centers comes out clean. Cool muffins in pans 5 minutes. Remove muffins from pans. Serve warm. Makes 12 muffins.

CHEDDAR-CORN ROLLS

4 to 4½ c. all-purpose flour
¾ c. yellow cornmeal
2 pkgs. active dry yeast
1¼ c. buttermilk
¼ c. sugar
3 T. butter or vegetable oil

3 T. Dijon-style mustard
2 tsp. salt
1 c. shredded sharp cheddar cheese
    (4 oz.)
2 eggs
1 recipe Roasted Red Pepper Butter

Combine 1½ cups of flour, cornmeal and yeast. Heat and stir buttermilk, sugar, butter, mustard and salt until lukewarm (120°). Add milk mixture, cheese and eggs to flour mixture. Beat with electric mixer on low speed 30 seconds, scraping bowl constantly. Beat 3 minutes on high speed. Using wooden spoon, stir in as much of remaining flour as you can. Turn dough out onto lightly floured surface. Knead in enough remaining flour to make stiff dough that is smooth and elastic, 6 to 8 minutes. Place dough in lightly greased bowl; turn once. Cover; let rise in warm place until double in size, about 1½ hours. Punch dough down. Turn out onto lightly floured surface. Halve dough. Cover; let rest 10 minutes. Grease 24 (2½-inch) muffin cups. Divide each dough half into 36 portions. Shape each portion into ball, pulling edges under to make smooth top. Place 3 balls in each prepared cup, smooth sides up. Cover; let rise in warm place until nearly double in size, about 45 minutes. Preheat oven to 375°. Bake 15 to 18 minutes, or until rolls sound hollow when lightly tapped. Immediately remove from muffin cups; cool slightly. Serve warm with Roasted Red Pepper Butter. Makes 24 rolls. **Roasted Red Pepper Butter:** Drain ¼ cup chopped bottles roasted red sweet peppers. Pat dry with paper towels. In food processor, combine peppers, ½ cup butter, softened and cut up and 1 clove garlic, minced. Cover and process until well mixed.

BLUE CHEESE HERB SPREAD

2 T. walnuts
2 T. chopped fresh parsley
2 T. chopped chives

½ c. blue cheese, crumbled
1 (8-oz.) pkg. cream cheese, cold

Place walnuts, parsley and chives in the bowl of a food processor and process until finely chopped. Place herb mixture in a small bowl and stir in blue cheese. Set aside. Place cream cheese in bowl of food processor and process until smooth. Add herb mixture to cream cheese and process until thoroughly blended. **Tips:** Spread can be made 3 days ahead and chilled, covered tightly. Serve at room temperature. This is great on pumpernickel bread or rye crackers. It's good on endive leaves, too, or as a sandwich filling with smoked ham.

EASY, NEVER-FAIL BUTTERMILK BISCUITS

Alice Banning

Self-rising flour

Buttermilk

Mix to soft dough stage. Roll on board with just enough flour to prevent sticking. Cut with cutter and put into pan with lots of melted shortening or oil. Coat both sides of biscuit in the oil and place on cookie sheet with sides touching. Bake on center rack at 425° approximately 20 minutes, or until golden brown and bottoms are crusty. Serve hot with butter.

BANANA BREAD

Christal Montgomery

3 lg. very ripe bananas
1 c. sugar
1 egg
½ c. butter, melted

1 ½ c. flour
¾ tsp. salt
¾ tsp. soda

Mash bananas with fork. Blend in sugar, egg and butter. Add flour, salt and soda. Mix well. Pour batter into greased and floured 9 x 5 x 3-inch loaf pan. Bake at 325° for approximately 1 hour. Makes 1 loaf. May add ½ cup nuts if desired.

YEAST ROLLS

Alice

1 c. warm water
2 pkgs. or 2 T. yeast

1 T. sugar

Mix well and set aside.

Mix in blender:

1 c. hot water
½ c. sugar
6 T. butter

1 T. salt
2 eggs
4 to 6 c. flour

Pour into large bowl. Add yeast mixture and mix. Add flour, 1 to 2 cups at a time, until firm enough to knead on floured board. Knead. Add flour a little at a time, until light and smooth. The less flour the better. Dough may be sticky. Oil bowl. Place dough to rise. When doubled, shape into rolls or loaf. Rise again in greased pans. Brush with butter. Bake at 350° for 15 to 20 minutes.

126207-15

DAD'S WORLD FAMOUS SANDWICHES

2 drops Tabasco sauce
1 ½ lbs. ground beef
2 eggs
½ c. chopped onions
½ c. chopped bell pepper
1 sm. bottle catsup

12 lg. sourdough rolls
1 tsp. onion powder
1 tsp. garlic salt
1 tsp. seasoned salt
2 c. mild cheddar cheese
2 c. sharp cheddar cheese

Preheat oven to 350°. Brown ground beef; drain grease and allow to cool. Split rolls, scoop out inside rolls. Save crumbs. In large bowl, put cooled meat, 2 eggs, ½ crumbs (savor, garlic salt, onion powder, salt and pepper to taste), catsup and 2 cups cheese. Mix thoroughly by hand. Add remaining cheese; mix thoroughly by hand. Add remaining cheese, onion and bell pepper. Should resemble cheese, onion and bell pepper. Should resemble stiff meat loaf. Add more bread crumbs if necessary. Fill scooped out rolls with meat mixture. Wrap in aluminum foil and seal. Place on cookie sheet and heat in preheated oven.

Recipe Favorites

126207-15

Desserts

Helpful Hints

- Keep eggs at room temperature to create greater volume when whipping egg whites for meringue.

- Pie dough can be frozen. Roll dough out between sheets of plastic wrap, stack in a pizza box, and keep the box in the freezer. Defrost in the fridge and use as needed. Use within 2 months.

- Place your pie plate on a cake stand when ready to flute the edges of the pie. The cake stand will make it easier to turn the pie plate, and you won't have to stoop over.

- When making decorative pie edges, use a spoon for a scalloped edge. Use a fork to make crosshatched and herringbone patterns.

- When cutting butter into flour for pastry dough, the process is easier if you cut the butter into small pieces before adding it to the flour.

- Pumpkin and other custard-style pies are done when they jiggle slightly in the middle. Fruit pies are done when the pastry is golden, juices bubble, and fruit is tender.

- Keep the cake plate clean while frosting by sliding 6-inch strips of waxed paper under each side of the cake. Once the cake is frosted and the frosting is set, pull the strips away, leaving a clean plate.

- Create a quick decorating tube to ice your cake with chocolate. Put chocolate in a heat-safe, zipper-lock plastic bag. Immerse it in simmering water until the chocolate is melted. Snip off the tip of one corner, and squeeze the chocolate out of the bag.

- Achieve professionally decorated cakes with a silky, molten look by blow-drying the frosting with a hair dryer until the frosting melts slightly.

- To ensure that you have equal amounts of batter in each pan when making a layered cake, use a kitchen scale to measure the weight.

- Prevent cracking in your cheesecake by placing a shallow pan of hot water on the bottom oven rack and keeping the oven door shut during baking.

- A cheesecake needs several hours to chill and set.

- For a perfectly cut cheesecake, dip the knife into hot water and clean it after each cut. You can also hold a length of dental floss taut and pull it down through the cheesecake to make a clean cut across the diameter of the cake.

DESSERTS

STRAWBERRY PIE
Lucy Bowen

**1 box crushed strawberries with 1
c. sugar**

3 T. cornstarch

Cook until thick and cool.

1 box whole strawberries

Sugar to taste

Put in baked pie shell and top with whipped cream. Refrigerate.

HELLO DOLLY
Alice Banning

1 cube margarine or butter
1 c. graham cracker crumbs
1 c. shredded coconut

1 c. chocolate chips
1 c. nuts
1 c. Eagle Brand milk

Layer ingredients in order called for except Eagle Brand milk. Cover with Eagle Brand milk. Bake at 375° for 30 minutes. Cool, cut into small squares. It's rich.

LEMON SURPRISE
Lilly Moore

Crust:

1 c. flour
1 cube melted margarine

½ c. nuts, chopped fine

Combine very well with fork. Place in bottom of 9 x 13-inch pan. Use hands to evenly spread. Bake at 350° for 30 minutes; let cool.

1st Layer:

8 oz. cream cheese, softened
¼ c. powdered sugar

8 oz. Cool Whip, slightly softened

Mix together. Then spread over crust.

2nd Layer:

**1 lg. pkg. lemon pudding, the kind
you bake**

Use directions for pie, except whip egg whites and fold in pudding as it cooks. **Third Layer:** Top with 8 ounces of Cool Whip. **Optional:** If you like chocolate, use chocolate instant pudding instead.

PISTACHIO LUSH

Robin Marshall

Crust:

1 ½ c. flour
1 ½ cubes margarine, melted

1 c. fine chopped nuts

Mix margarine, flour and nuts in a 4-quart or 9 x 13-inch pan and bake at 325° for 30 minutes. Cool.

1st Layer:

1 (8 oz.) cream cheese
1 c. powdered sugar

1 ½ c. Cool Whip (12 oz.)

Soften cream cheese and mix with sugar and Cool Whip. Spread on cooled crust.

2nd Layer:

2 sm. instant pistachio pudding

3 c. cold milk

Heat until thick. Spread on top of cream cheese mixture. **3rd Layer:** Spread on remaining Cool Whip from 12-ounce container. Sprinkle with chopped nuts.

BUTTERFINGER ICE CREAM PIE

Rhonda Pierce

6 Butterfinger candy bars, crushed
½ gal. French vanilla or vanilla ice
  cream

9-inch graham cracker crust
1 sm. Cool Whip

Put candy bars in a plastic zip bag. Smash all the candy bars into little tiny pieces with a hammer. Let the ice cream get soft, not melted. Mix thoroughly with candy bars and ice cream, then pour into graham cracker shell. **Optional:** Add Cool Whip on top and sprinkle a little of the candy bars on the top for decoration. Place in the freezer until frozen, approximately 2 hours, and then eat.

SIMPLE PEACH COBBLER

Janice Pelham

6 lg. peaches, sliced thin
¼ c. sugar

1 T. lemon juice
1 tsp. cornstarch

Dough:

1 c. flour
½ c. sugar
½ tsp. salt
1 tsp. baking powder

¾ stick cold butter, cut into sm.
  pieces
¼ c. boiling water

Preheat oven to 425°. Toss peaches, sugar, lemon juice and cornstarch in an 8 x 8-inch baking dish, tart pan or similar. Bake in oven for 10 minutes. While peaches are cooking, combine flour, sugar, salt and baking powder. Add cold butter and with a pastry blender or your fingertips, combine. The texture should be that of coarse cornmeal. Add boiling water and mix until just combined. When peaches are done, drop tablespoons of dough on top of peaches. It will not cover the whole dish, but dough will spread as it bakes. Great!

126207-15

APPLE DUMPLINGS
Janice McWhorter

1 can crescent rolls	1 Granny Smith apple

Peel apple. Cut in 8 pieces. Wrap crescent roll around each wedge of apple. Place in a buttered baking dish. Melt 1 stick of butter in pan. Add:

1 c. sugar	Pinch of nutmeg
1 T. cinnamon	1 tsp. vanilla

Heat. Then add ½ can Mountain Dew. Pour over apples and bake at 350° until brown, about 25 minutes. Spoon mixture over top. Serve with whipped cream or ice cream. If you use the larger crescent rolls, cut apple into 4 pieces.

GRANDMA MAXINE ROBISON'S FRUIT COCKTAIL CAKE

1 (30 oz.) fruit cocktail in heavy syrup	½ tsp. baking soda
2 c. all-purpose flour	1 c. sugar

Mix together ingredients well and pour into a buttered iron skillet. Bake in a preheated 350° oven, until golden brown.

Topping:

1 c. evaporated milk	1 cube butter
1 c. sugar	

Mix together in saucepan. Bring to a boil for 1 minute and pour all over top of cake.

MOUNTAIN DEW APPLE DUMPLINGS

3 cans Pillsbury crescent rolls	1 tsp. cinnamon
3 Mrs. Smith apples	12-oz. can Mountain Dew
2 sticks butter	1 tsp. nutmeg
1 ½ c. sugar	

Core and peel apples. Cut each into 8 wedges. Roll each apple in a crescent roll and place in baking dish. Melt butter, sugar and cinnamon; mix well. Pour over apples and roll in a baking dish. Add Mountain Dew. Bake at 350° for 45 minutes. Will be floating when you put in oven. May also be when take out, but will settle as cools. Preparation time: 15 minutes.

GINGERBREAD MEN
Rhonda Pierce

3 c. sifted flour	½ tsp. salt
1 ½ tsp. ginger	⅓ c. brown sugar, firmly packed
⅔ c. molasses	⅓ c. butter or margarine or other shortening
1 egg, unbeaten	
3 tsp. baking powder	

(continued)

Measure flour, baking powder, ginger and salt into sifter. Cream butter until soft in medium-size bowl. Add brown sugar gradually, creaming after each addition until well blended. Beat in molasses and egg. Sift and add dry ingredients to creamed mixture; blend well. Cover bowl. Chill dough for 2 hours, or until firm enough to roll. Grease cookie sheets. Roll out chilled dough, a small amount at a time, to 1/8-inch thickness on lightly floured pastry cloth or board. Cut out cookies with floured gingerbread man cutter or around paper pattern as a guide. With tip of pointed knife, transfer cookies with wide spatula or pancake turner to prepared cookie sheet. Bake at 350° for 8 minutes, or until crisp. Run spatula under cookies to loosen from cookie sheets. Remove to wire cake racks and cool. Make faces and button fronts with candy decorations, currants or icing.

COOL, NO-COOK BANANA CREAM CHEESE FILLING
Betty Gallagher

1 stick Betty Crocker Instant Mixing Pie Crust Mix
3 med. sized bananas
1 (8-oz.) pkg. Borden's cream cheese, softened to room temp.

1 1/3 c. (15-oz. can) Eagle Brand condensed milk
1/3 c. lemon juice
1 tsp. vanilla extract

Prepare 9-inch baked pie shell as directed on the pie crust mix package. Cool. Slice 2 of the bananas, line your pie shell. Whip softened cream cheese until light and fluffy. Gradually beat in sweetened condensed milk until well blended. Add lemon juice and vanilla extract and blend well. Pour into the prepared crust. Chill for about 2 hours or until firm. Slice third banana; garnish pie. Decorate with fresh mint leaves if desired and serve to 6 delighted people.

EASY PINEAPPLE UPSIDE-DOWN CAKE
Louise Cowell

1 yellow cake mix
2 T. butter
1/3 c. pineapple juice
3/4 c. brown sugar

1 can sliced pineapple
1/4 c. chopped nuts (pecans or walnuts)

Melt butter over low heat in 9 x 13-inch pan. Add brown sugar to butter to dissolve. Add pineapple juice to mixture. Cook over low heat until syrup consistency. Take pan off stove. Cut pineapple slices and arrange in pan of syrup. Add nuts if desired. Set pan aside. Make cake as per directions for 9 x 13-inch cake. Pour over pineapple mixture in pan. Bake as directed for 9 x 13-inch cake. When cake is done, transfer immediately to cake plate or board by putting plate or board on top of cake and turning upside down, having cake wind up on plate or board. Pineapple should be on top. **Tip:** If cake is not transferred immediately from hot oven, it will stick to bottom of pan.

PANIC CAKE
Joyce Goodwin

1 can pie filling
1 sm. box cake mix

1/2 c. melted margarine
1/2 c. chopped nuts

(continued)

126207-15

Pour pie filling into greased pan. Sprinkle cake mix over the filling. Pour melted margarine over cake mix. Top with nuts. Bake at 325° for 35 minutes to 1 hour, depending on the size of the pan. Serve with whipped cream or vanilla ice cream. **Suggested Combinations:** While cake mix with cherry, blueberry or peach filling. Spice cake mix with apple filling. Yellow cake with pineapple filling.

CHOCOLATE ECLAIR CAKE
Dolly Barton

2 c. sugar
½ c. milk
⅔ c. cocoa

2 sticks butter
2 tsp. vanilla

Bring these ingredients to a boil. Cook 1 minute and let cool.

1 pkg. graham crackers (I use 1 ½ pkgs.)
1 lg. box instant vanilla pudding

3 c. milk
8 oz. Cool Whip

Mix pudding and add to Cool Whip. Cover bottom of 9 x 13-inch pan with graham crackers (just enough to cover). Pour pudding mixture over graham crackers. Use remaining graham crackers to layer the top of the pudding. Pour cooled chocolate mixture over the top. Allow to sit in refrigerator overnight.

OATMEAL PIE
Betty Gallagher

¾ c. oatmeal, uncooked
¾ c. dark Karo syrup
¾ c. canned milk
½ c. white sugar

½ c. butter (1 stick)
1 c. coconut
2 eggs, well beaten

Mix all ingredients together and pour into an unbaked pie shell and bake at 350° for 40 to 45 minutes.

LEMON PIE
Linda Conner

1 sm. can thawed lemonade
1 (9 oz.) Cool Whip

½ can Eagle Brand milk
1 (9-inch) graham cracker crust

Mix lemonade, Cool Whip and Eagle Brand milk together. Pour into crust. Chill. **Tip:** Lemonade can be substituted with any other frozen fruit, like grapefruit!

REESE'S PEANUT BUTTER PIE
Robin Marshall

3 egg yolks
¾ c. sugar
2 ½ c. milk
1 tsp. salt

¼ c. cornstarch
1 tsp. vanilla
¾ c. powdered sugar
½ c. peanut butter

Mix powdered sugar and peanut butter until crumbly; set aside. In a mixing bowl, add 3 egg yolks, sugar, milk, ⅛ teaspoon salt, cornstarch, 1 tablespoon of peanut butter and vanilla. Mix well and place into a double boiler. Bring to a boil, approximately 1 minute. Into a cool pie crust, add half of the peanut butter and

(continued)

half of the powdered sugar. Pour in the pie filling. Let cool. Add other half of peanut butter and powdered sugar. Add chocolate shavings.

ROBIN'S BROWNIES
Robin Marshall

¾ c. all-purpose flour	2 eggs, beaten
¼ tsp. salt	1 tsp. vanilla
½ c. butter	¼ c. cocoa
1 c. sugar	¾ c. chopped nuts

Mix all ingredients together. Place into buttered brownie pan. Bake for 20 minutes at 350°.

PEACH CAKE
Lucy Bowen

1 box yellow cake mix	½ tsp. lemon extract
1 can peach pie mix filling	½ c. nuts (opt.)
3 eggs	

Combine cake mix, pie filling and eggs. Blend until completely moist, 3 minutes. Bake at 350° for 45 minutes.

IMPOSSIBLE PECAN PIE
Joyce Goodwin

1 ½ c. chopped pecans	¾ c. packed brown sugar
¾ c. milk	¾ c. dark corn syrup
½ c. Bisquick baking mix	¼ c. softened butter
4 eggs	1 ½ tsp. vanilla

Heat oven to 350°. Grease 10 x 1 ½-inch pie plate. Sprinkle pecans in plate. Beat remaining ingredients until smooth (15 seconds in blender on high or 1 minute with hand beater). Pour into plate. Bake until knife inserted in center comes out clean, 50 to 55 minutes. Cool 5 minutes.

SCRIPTURE CAKE
Lucy Bowen

Gen. 18:8 (¾ c. butter)	II Chron. 9:9 (¼ tsp. nutmeg,
Jer. 6:20 (1 ½ c. sugar)	cloves, allspice)
Isa. 10:15 (5 eggs, separated)	Judg. 4:19 (½ c. milk)
Lev. 24:5 (3 c. flour)	Gen. 43:11 (¾ c. chopped almonds)
II Kings 2:20 (¾ tsp. salt)	Jer. 24:5 (¾ c. dried figs)
Amos 4:5 (3 tsp. baking powder)	II Sam. 16:1 (¾ c. raisins)
Ex. 30:23 (1 tsp. cinnamon)	

Cream butter with sugar. Beat in yolks of eggs, one at a time. Sift flour, baking powder and spices. Blend into creamed mixture alternately with milk. Beat egg whites until stiff. Fold in almonds, figs and raisins. Turn into 10-inch tube pan that has been greased and floured. Bake at 325° for 1 hour and 10 minutes. Cool, remove from pan. Serve with Burnt Sugar Syrup.

(continued)

64

Burnt Sugar Syrup:

Jer. 6:20 (1 ½ c. sugar) **Gen. 18:8 (¼ c. butter)**
Gen. 24:25 (½ c. water)

Melt sugar in heavy skillet over low heat. Continue cooking until syrup is deep amber. Add water. Cook until syrup is smooth. Remove from heat. Add butter. Stir until melted. Cool. Makes 1 ½ cups.

EARTHQUAKE CAKE
Joyce Goodwin

1 ½ c. pecans, chopped
1 ½ c. flaked coconut
1 pkg. German chocolate cake mix
1 stick butter, room temp.

1 (8-oz.) pkg. cream cheese, room temp.
1 (16-oz.) pkg. confectioners' sugar
1 tsp. vanilla

Spray a 9 x 13 x 2-inch pan with Pam and sprinkle pecans and coconut on the bottom. Mix cake mix according to directions and pour over pecans and coconut. Mix together butter, cream cheese, confectioners' sugar and vanilla. Drop in small or large blobs on top of cake mix. Bake at 350° until done.

DUMP CAKE
Joyce Goodwin

1 (16-oz.) can fruit cocktail with juice
1 layer cake mix

¼ c. brown sugar
¼ c. butter, melted

In an 8- or 9-inch cake pan, dump fruit cocktail with juice. Sprinkle cake mix over fruit cocktail. Sprinkle brown sugar over cake mix. Pour butter over cake mix and brown sugar. Do not stir. Bake at 350° for 30 to 45 minutes. Make servings small as cake is very rich. Top with whipped cream.

PECAN PIE
Robin Marshall

6 eggs
1 ⅓ tsp. sugar
⅔ tsp. salt
⅔ c. melted butter

2 c. corn syrup
2 tsp. vanilla
2 c. chopped pecans

Combine all ingredients until smooth and pour in shells. Bake until set for 40 to 45 minutes at 350°.

LEMONADE PIE
Alice Banning

1 (8-oz.) tub Cool Whip
½ c. lemon juice
1 T. vanilla

1 can sweetened condensed milk
1 graham cracker crust

Mix all together until creamy and pour into crust. Chill.

MARSHMALLOW PIE
Robin

Crescent rolls, as many as you want to roll up
Lg. marshmallows, one for each crescent roll
Cinnamon and sugar mixture (about ½ c. for each 2 pkgs. of crescent rolls)

Melted butter or oleo, about 1 c. for each 2 pkgs. of crescent rolls

Separate the crescent rolls. Dip a marshmallow in the melted butter, then roll into the cinnamon and sugar mixture. Place each dipped marshmallow at the large end of a crescent roll and then proceed to roll up, making sure that all openings are sealed. Dip the small end back into the melted butter, then place in a baking dish. After all crescents and marshmallows are rolled up and in the baking dish, dab the remaining melted butter over the top of the crescents and then sprinkle the remaining cinnamon and sugar mixture over the top of them and bake at 400° until golden brown. While the pie is baking, make a glaze out of powdered sugar and milk mixture. This will be very runny, then drizzle over the top of the hot rolls just as you take them out of the oven. Eat and enjoy.

NEW PECAN PIE
Joyce Goodwin

4 eggs
1 ⅓ tsp. baking powder
14 single graham crackers, crushed
Whipped cream

1 c. pecans
1 c. sugar
1 tsp. vanilla

Beat egg whites and baking powder until stiff. Add sugar and vanilla. Fold in pecans and graham crackers. Pour in well greased baking dish. Bake for 30 to 40 minutes at 375°. Refrigerate for 3 to 4 hours. Top with whipped cream.

APPLE CRISP FOR TWO
Edna Welch

2 lg. tart apples, peeled and sliced
1 T. lemon juice
2 T. brown sugar
2 T. quick cooking oats

2 T. butter or margarine, melted
Dash of ground cinnamon
Whipped cream or vanilla ice cream (opt.)

Place apples in an ungreased 2- or 3-cup baking dish. Sprinkle with lemon juice. Combine brown sugar, oats, butter and cinnamon. Sprinkle over apples. Cover and bake at 350° for 30 minutes. Uncover and bake 15 minutes longer, or until apples are tender. Serve with whipped cream or ice cream if desired. Yields 2 servings.

126207-15

S'MORES CAKE

Cake:

2 ⅓ c. all-purpose flour
½ c. unsweetened cocoa powder
1 tsp. baking soda
½ tsp. salt
1 c. (2 sticks) unsalted butter, softened

2 c. granulated sugar
4 lg. eggs
1 c. milk, mixed with 1 T. white vinegar
1 T. vanilla extract

Filling & Topping:

1 ½ c. confectioners' sugar
1 ½ c. marshmallow creme
¼ c. (½ stick) unsalted butter, softened

2 (11.75-oz.) jars hot fudge topping
2 graham cracker boards, crushed
1 ½ c. mini marshmallows

Heat oven to 350°. Coat 3 (9-inch) round cake pans with nonstick spray for baking. **Cake:** In a medium bowl, whisk together flour, cocoa, baking soda and salt. In a large bowl with an electric mixer, beat butter until smooth. Add sugar and beat for 2 minutes, until light and fluffy. Beat in eggs, one at a time. On low speed, beat in half the flour mixture, then the milk mixture, followed by remaining flour mixture. Stir in vanilla and divide batter among prepared pans. Bake at 350° for 30 to 35 minutes, or until cake springs back when lightly pressed. Cool in pans on wire racks for 10 minutes. Run a thin knife around edge of pans; turn cakes out of pans and cool completely. **Filling:** While cake layers cool, combine confectioners' sugar, marshmallow creme, butter and ½ teaspoon water in a bowl. Beat on low speed until blended and a good spreading consistency. Once cakes have cooled, place one cake layer on a plate. Spread top with ⅔ cup of the fudge topping. Sprinkle with 1 tablespoon of the crushed graham crackers. Spread a second cake layer with half the marshmallow frosting, then invert onto cake layer on platter. Spread top with ⅔ cup of the fudge topping and carefully spread with remaining marshmallow filling (may look marbled). Sprinkle with 1 tablespoon crushed graham crackers. Spread remaining layer with remaining ⅔ cup fudge sauce (do not stack onto cake yet). Sprinkle with remaining crushed graham crackers and top with marshmallows. Arrange oven rack so cake layer can be about 3 to 4 inches from the heat source*. Heat broiler. Broil marshmallows for 30 seconds, until they just begin to brown. Carefully place layer on cake. *You may use a creme brulee torch. Makes 16 servings. Preparation time: 30 minutes.

ALMOND POPPY SEED CAKE   Betty Montgomery

1 ¼ c. sugar
⅓ c. safflower oil
2 T. poppy seed
2 eggs
¼ tsp. salt

¾ tsp. almond flavor (extract)
1 ½ c. flour
½ tsp. baking powder
½ c. milk
1 c. sliced almonds

Combine first 6 ingredients. Add flour and baking powder, mixed, while adding milk. Pour into large greased loaf pan (can use glass bake pan). Sprinkle sliced almonds all over top and softly fork into batter. Don't smash nuts all the way in. Bake at 350° for 1 ¼ hours in loaf pan used. Bake 35 to 40 minutes if flat pan used.

OATMEAL TRAIL CAKE

Cake:

1 c. quick cooking oatmeal
1 ½ c. hot tap water
½ c. oil
½ c. brown sugar (Baking Splenda)
½ c. white sugar (Baking Splenda)
2 eggs

1 tsp. vanilla
1 ½ c. flour
1 tsp. baking soda
1 tsp. cinnamon
1 pinch of nutmeg
½ tsp. salt

Icing:

1 stick butter, melted
½ c. brown sugar (Splenda Baking)
2 T. evaporated canned milk

½ c. chopped nuts
1 c. unsweetened shredded coconut
   or coconut chips

Cake: Pour water over oats in a separate bowl and let stand while mixing other ingredients. Mix together other cake ingredients, then pour in oatmeal mixture and mix thoroughly. Bake in greased (Pam is fine) 9 x 13-inch pan at 350° for 25 to 30 minutes. **Icing:** Mix together and spread over hot cake. Return to oven under broiler for 3 to 4 minutes, or until frosting begins to bubble and turn brown. **FYI:** Do not walk away from the oven while you are broiling the frosting (been there, done that, oops). Keep your eye on it because it scorches easily.

CARROT CAKE

Lilly, Suzzie & Cherrie Moore

4 c. sifted flour
4 c. sugar
4 tsp. cinnamon
4 tsp. baking powder
1 ½ tsp. baking soda
4 c. grated carrots
4 tsp. vanilla
1 tsp. salt

6 eggs
2 c. chopped nuts
1 ½ c. oil
1 ½ c. buttermilk
2 sm. cans crushed pineapple, well
   drained
1 (7-oz.) pkg. coconut

Preheat oven to 350°. Sift dry ingredients together. Beat eggs, oil, sugar, buttermilk and vanilla. Mix well, then add to dry ingredients. Mix in pineapple, carrots, nuts and coconut. Pour into a lightly greased and floured pan. Bake 55 minutes.

Icing:

2 c. sugar
2 cubes butter or ½ lb.
2 T. white corn syrup

1 c. buttermilk
2 tsp. vanilla

Mix all ingredients together except vanilla. Boil 5 minutes. Remove and add vanilla. Pour over hot cake.

SINFULLY SWEET CHOCOLATE CAKE

Rhonda Pierce

1 chocolate cake mix
1 c. pecans, chopped (opt.)
1 bottle caramel syrup

1 med. Cool Whip bowl
1 sm. can condensed sweet milk
1 Hershey's milk chocolate bar

Follow directions on cake mix box but add nuts to mix. Pull out of oven. Poke holes with a fork. Pour Caramel Syrup into same holes. Let cool for 10 to 20 minutes on counter or in refrigerator. Once cool, put Cool Whip all over top of cake. Take potato peeler and shred the chocolate bar all over the top of the Cool Whip. Put cake in refrigerator for at least 30 minutes or longer before you serve it.

LAZY DAISY CAKE

Sandra Kester

2 beaten egg
1 tsp. vanilla
1 tsp. baking powder
1 T. butter

1 c. sugar
1 c. flour
¼ tsp. salt
½ c. milk

Beat together eggs, sugar and vanilla; beat well. Sift together flour, baking powder and salt, then add to egg mixture. Heat ½ cup milk with 1 tablespoon butter. Beat slowly into mixture. This will be very thin. Do not add any more flour. Pour this mixture into a sprayed 8-inch square pan. Double for larger cake. Bake ½ hour in 350° oven, then spread this mixture over warm cake.

3 T. melted butter
2 T. canned milk
½ c. nuts, chopped

5 T. brown sugar
½ c. coconut

Frosting: Mix together all the ingredients in a saucepan. Cook for 3 to 5 minutes. Spread over cake.

APPLE BUNDT CAKE

Betty Montgomery

2 c. flour
1 ½ c. sugar
1 tsp. cinnamon
1 tsp. baking powder
½ c. applesauce
3 eggs

3 apples, chopped
1 c. chopped pecans
1 tsp. soda
½ tsp. salt
½ c. (1 stick) butter, melted

Butter and flour bundt pan. In a bowl, mix together flour, sugar, cinnamon, baking powder, applesauce, apples, pecans, soda, salt and melted butter. Pour into bundt pan. Bake at 350° for 60 minutes. Cool for 30 minutes. Turn out onto a plate while still warm; sprinkle powdered sugar onto cake.

PIE CRUST NEVER FAIL RECIPE

James and Marilyn

1 c. shortening, cold
1 tsp. salt or to taste
3 c. flour

Ice water, enough to stick dough
    together

(continued)

With fingers, crumble flour, salt and shortening together quickly, less handling for tender flaky crust. Drizzle ice water into crumbled flour just until it sticks together, enough to roll out. Flour board and roll thin. Put in pie plate and bake at 350° until brown, about 15 to 20 minutes.

PINEAPPLE RICE PUDDING

Edna Welch

1 c. cooked rice
1 (8-oz.) can crushed pineapple, drained
½ c. whipping cream

2 T. confectioners' sugar
¼ tsp. vanilla extract
Maraschino cherries
Fresh mint (opt.)

In a small bowl, combine the rice and pineapple; set aside in a small mixing bowl. Beat cream, sugar and vanilla until soft peaks form. Fold into rice mixture. Cover and chill until ready to serve. Garnish with cherries and mint if desired.

COCA-COLA CAKE

Lilly, Suzzie & Cherrie Moore

Mix 2 cups of flour and 2 cups of sugar. In large pan, put 2 cubes of margarine, 3 tablespoons cocoa and cup Coke in a pan. Boil. Pour over flour and sugar. Mix well. Add ½ cup buttermilk, 1 tablespoon vanilla and 2 eggs. Beat well. Add 1½ cups marshmallows and mix. Pour in pans. If you use self-rising flour, don't use 1½ teaspoons soda or salt.

Frosting:

1 cube margarine
3 T. cocoa

6 T. cake

Boil together, then pour over 1 pound of powdered sugar. Mix well. Add 1 teaspoon vanilla and ½ cup nuts.

126207-15

Cookies & Candy

Helpful Hints

- Unbaked cookie dough can be covered and refrigerated for up to 24 hours or frozen in an airtight container for up to 9 months.

- Bake one cookie sheet at a time on the middle oven rack.

- Decorate cookies with chocolate by placing cookies on a rack over waxed paper. Dip the tines of a fork into melted chocolate and wave the fork gently back and forth to make line decorations.

- Some cookies need indentations on top to fill with jam or chocolate. Use the rounded end of a honey dipper.

- Dip cookie cutters in flour or powdered sugar and shake off excess before cutting. For chocolate dough, dip cutters in baking cocoa.

- Tin coffee cans make excellent freezer containers for cookies.

- If you only have one cookie sheet on hand, line it with parchment paper. While one batch is baking, load a second sheet of parchment paper to have another batch ready to bake. Cleanup will be easier.

- When a recipe calls for packed brown sugar, fill the correct size measuring cup with sugar and use one cup size smaller to pack the brown sugar into its cup.

- Cut-up dried fruit often sticks to the blade of your knife. To prevent this problem, coat the blade of your knife with a thin film of vegetable spray before cutting.

- Instead of folding nuts into brownie batter, sprinkle on top of batter before baking. This keeps nuts crunchy instead of soggy.

- Only use glass or shiny metal pans. Dark or nonstick pans will cause brownies to become soggy and low in volume.

- When making bars, line pan with aluminum foil and prepare as directed. The bars can be lifted out, and cleanup is easy.

- Cutting bars is easier if you score the bars right as the pan leaves the oven. When the bars cool, cut along the scored lines.

- Use a double boiler for melting chocolate to prevent it from scorching. A slow cooker on the lowest setting also works well for melting chocolate, especially when coating a large amount of candy.

- Parchment paper provides an excellent nonstick surface for candy. Waxed paper should not be used for high-temperature candy.

COOKIES & CANDY

PEANUT BUTTER COOKIES   Mike Barton

½ c. butter or margarine
½ c. peanut butter
½ c. granulated sugar
½ c. brown sugar
1 egg

½ tsp. vanilla
1 ¼ c. sifted all-purpose flour
¾ tsp. soda
¼ tsp. salt

Thoroughly cream butter, peanut butter, sugars, egg and vanilla. Sift together dry ingredients; blend into creamed mixture. Shape into 1-inch balls. Roll in granulated sugar. Place 2 inches apart on ungreased cookie sheet. Press 5 peanut halves atop each or crisscross with fork tines. Bake at 357° for 10 to 12 minutes. Cool slightly. Remove from pan. Makes 4 dozen.

KARI'S OATMEAL COOKIES   Kari Blackburn

1 c. butter, softened
1 c. sugar
1 tsp. vanilla
2 ½ c. oatmeal
1 tsp. soda
12 oz. chocolate chips or 6 oz. vanilla chips and 6 oz. chocolate chips

1 plain Hershey's candy bar, chopped or grated
2 eggs
1 c. brown sugar
2 c. flour
½ tsp. salt
1 tsp. baking powder
1 ½ c. chopped nuts

Cream butter and both sugars together. Add eggs and vanilla, then mix well. Add flour, oatmeal, salt, soda and baking powder together. Add to butter and egg mixture, stirring well. Add Hershey's candy bar. Mix in nuts and chocolate (vanilla) chips. Chill about 5 minutes. Drop mixture about the size of a golf ball on a cookie sheet. Place about 2 inches apart. Bake at 350° for 8 to 10 minutes.

MISSOURI COOKIES   Gerri Johnson

2 c. sugar
6 T. cocoa
½ c. milk
1 stick margarine

3 c. oatmeal
½ c. peanut butter
½ tsp. vanilla
Wax paper

Mix together sugar, cocoa, milk and margarine in medium to large saucepan. Stir while waiting for margarine to melt and begins to boil. When it starts to boil, stir for 1 minute. Remove from heat, then add remaining ingredients. Stir and spoon onto wax paper. Let sit until cool.

CHOCOLATE CHIP "SURPRISE" COOKIES

Louise Cowell

¾ c. butter or margarine
¾ c. sugar
¾ c. brown sugar
2 eggs
1 c. chopped nuts
2 ½ c. flour

1 tsp. soda
1 tsp. salt
1 tsp. vanilla
6 oz. chocolate chips
6 oz. vanilla chips "surprise"

Mix flour, soda and salt; set aside. Mix butter and both sugars together and beat until creamy. Add eggs and mix well. Add vanilla. Add nuts and chocolate and vanilla chips; mix well. Slowly add the dry ingredients to the mixture, stirring well. Place in refrigerator for approximately 5 minutes. Drop by large tablespoons on cookie sheet. Bake in preheated oven at 350° for 10 to 12 minutes. Cool for about 5 minutes before storing. Put in sealed container with one slice of bread. This will keep cookies moist.

EASY CHOCOLATE COOKIES

Edna Welch

1 pkg. white cake mix
½ c. cooking oil
2 T. water
2 eggs

½ c. chopped nuts
1 c. (6-oz. pkg.) semi-sweet
    chocolate chips

Preheat oven to 350°. Blend cake mix, oil, water and eggs. Stir in chips and nuts. Drop from a teaspoon onto ungreased cookie sheet. Bake for 10 to 12 minutes. Tops of cookies will look pale. Cool on cookie sheet for 1 minute, then remove to rack or waxed paper. One-half cup of applesauce may be substituted for oil to cut fat and cholesterol.

CHOCOLATE COOKIES

Louise Cowell

4 (1-oz.) squares unsweetened
    chocolate
½ c. oil
2 c. sugar
4 eggs
2 tsp. vanilla

2 c. flour
2 tsp. baking powder
½ tsp. salt
¾ c. chopped nuts
1 c. powdered sugar

Melt chocolate over hot water. Add oil and sugar. Beat in eggs, one at a time. Mix well, then add vanilla. Mix flour, baking powder and salt together. Gradually add this to the chocolate mixture. Mix well, then add chopped nuts. Chill dough for about 1 hour. Roll dough into medium-size balls. Then roll balls in the powdered sugar. Place balls on greased cookie sheet. Bake at 350° for about 12 minutes.

126207-15

CHOCOLATE CHIP "SURPRISE" COOKIES

Louise Cowell

¾ c. butter or margarine
¾ c. brown sugar
6 oz. chocolate chips
6 oz. vanilla chips "Surprise"
¾ c. sugar
1 c. chopped nuts
1 tsp. soda
1 tsp. salt
2 eggs
2 ½ c. flour
1 tsp. vanilla

Mix flour, soda and salt, then set aside. Mix butter and both sugars together and beat until creamy. Add eggs and mix well. Add vanilla, then nuts, chocolate and vanilla chips. Mix well. Slowly add dry ingredients to the mixture, stirring well. Place in refrigerator for approximately 5 minutes. Drop large tablespoons on cookie sheet. Bake in preheated oven at 350° for 10 to 12 minutes. Cool for about 5 minutes before storing. Put in sealed container with 1 slice of bread. This will keep cookies moist.

CHOCOLATE MOUSSE CONES

1 (12-oz.) bag semisweet chocolate chips
¼ c. solid vegetable shortening
12 sm. ice cream cones (3-oz. pkg.)
1 pkg. cook & serve chocolate pudding mix
1 (.25-oz.) env. unflavored gelatin
4 oz. cream cheese softened
2 c. 1% milk
1 tsp. almond extract
1 c. heavy cream
2 T. chopped sliced almonds (opt.)

Combine chocolate chips and shortening in a glass bowl. Microwave for 1 minute, then stir until smooth. With a small brush, coat insides of cones with some melted chocolate. Turn cones upside down on a rack over a sheet of wax paper and let harden in refrigerator. Whisk together pudding mix and gelatin in a medium saucepan. Whisk in milk. Cook, stirring, over medium heat for 8 to 10 minutes, until pudding comes to a full boil. Remove from heat and stir in almond extract. Cool at room temperature for 20 minutes, stirring occasionally. In a medium bowl, beat cream cheese with an electric mixer until very smooth. Add heavy cream and sugar and beat until medium peaks are formed. Fold ⅓ of the cream cheese mixture into cooled pudding mixture to lighten. Fold in remaining cream cheese mixture and transfer to a large piping bag. Snip off corner of the bag. Flip over cones and place them in a cupcake pan to help balance them. Pipe mousse into cones, dividing equally. Refrigerate for 20 minutes. Reheat chocolate in microwave for 30 seconds. Dip cones into melted chocolate. **Optional:** Sprinkle half with chopped almonds.

PEANUT BUTTER FUDGE

Lilly, Suzzie & Cherrie Moore

Melt together 1 ½ cubes margarine and 2 cups of peanut butter. Lay in pan and push down with fingers. Top with 1 box of powdered sugar. Melt together in double boiler: 2 (8-ounce) Hershey's bars and ⅓ bar Parawax. Pour Hershey's mixture over peanut butter. Cool. Cut into squares.

CARNATION FIVE-MINUTE FUDGE
Betty Gallagher

Combine ⅔ cup undiluted Carnation evaporated milk, 2 tablespoons butter and 1⅔ cups sugar in saucepan. Heat to boiling. Cook 5 minutes, stirring constantly. Remove from heat. Add 2 cups miniature marshmallows, ½ cup chopped nuts, 1½ cups semi-sweet chocolate bits and 1 teaspoon vanilla. Stir until marshmallows are melted. Pour into buttered 8- or 9-inch square pan. Garnish with nuts if desired. Cool. Cut into squares.

HOMEMADE ICE CREAM
Rhonda Pierce

3 eggs	**3 or 4 T. vanilla**
Regular milk	**1¾ c. sugar**
1 can condensed milk	**¼ tsp. salt**

In a large mixing bowl, mix 1 quart of milk and 1 cup of sugar. When mixed well, pour into ice cream container. Use same bowl and beat 3 eggs. Add ¾ cup sugar, vanilla and condensed milk. When mixed well, add 1 quart of milk. Add half of the last quart of milk slowly. Pour this into ice cream container. If container is not full enough, add enough milk to bring it almost to the top. Leave enough space at top for ice cream to freeze. Put container in freezer. Add ice and salt alternately. Plug in freezer or turn manually until it won't turn any more. Makes 4 quarts of homemade ice cream. **Optional:** Can add chocolate chips, strawberries, peaches, nuts or your favorite additional ingredient at "when mixed well" instructions.

GINGERBREAD MEN
Rhonda Pierce

3 c. sifted flour	**3 tsp. baking powder**
1½ tsp. ginger	**½ tsp. salt**
⅔ c. molasses	**⅓ c. brown sugar, firmly packed**
1 egg, unbeaten	**⅓ c. butter**

Measure flour, baking powder, ginger and salt into a sifter. Cream butter until soft in medium-size bowl. Add brown sugar gradually, creaming after each addition until well blended. Beat in molasses and egg. Sift and add dry ingredients to creamed mixture. Blend well. Cover bowl; chill dough for 2 hours, or until firm enough to roll. Grease cookie sheets. Roll out chilled dough, a small amount at a time, to a ⅛-inch thickness on lightly floured pastry cloth or board. Cut out cookies with floured gingerbread man cutter or around paper pattern as a guide with the tip of pointed knife, transfer cookies with wide spatula or pancake turner to prepared cookie sheet. Bake at 350° for 8 minutes, or until crisp. Run spatula under cookies to loosen from cookie sheets. Remove to wire cake racks to cool. Make faces and button fronts with candy decorations, currants of icing.

CHOCOLATE PEANUT BUTTER CUP COOKIES

1 (16.5-oz.) pkg. refrigerated peanut butter cookie dough	**Mini muffin pan**
1 (24-count) bag miniature chocolate-peanut butter chips	

(continued)

126207-15

Preheat oven to 350°. Slice cookie dough into 1-inch thick slices, then into quarters. Place ¼ into each cup of a mini muffin pan. Bake for 9 to 11 minutes. While the dough is still warm, push a peanut butter cup into each muffin cup and let cool in the pan. Use a spoon to remove them.

PINTO BEAN COOKIES

1 c. sugar or 1 c. light brown sugar and ½ c. white sugar or 1 c. Splenda
1 (3 ⅛-oz.) pkg. sugar free vanilla pudding
½ c. oil
2 c. flour
½ tsp. cloves
1 tsp. nutmeg
½ c. unsweetened applesauce
¾ c. mashed pinto beans
1 c. pecans, chopped
1 egg
½ tsp. salt
1 tsp. cinnamon
1 tsp. baking soda
1 c. raisins
½ tsp. vanilla

Cream sugar, vanilla pudding and oil together. Add baking soda to applesauce. Mix applesauce, pinto beans and vanilla to sugar mixture. Add beaten egg. Stir in nuts and raisins. Drop by spoonfuls on greased cookie sheet. Bake at 350° for about 15 minutes, or until golden brown.

SNICKERS SURPRISES

2 sticks margarine, softened
1 c. creamy peanut butter
2 eggs
3 ½ c. all-purpose flour, sifted
½ tsp. salt
1 c. light brown sugar
1 c. sugar
1 tsp. vanilla
1 tsp. baking soda
1 pkg. Snickers miniatures

Combine the margarine, peanut butter and sugars using a mixture on medium to low speed until light and fluffy. Slowly add eggs and vanilla until thoroughly blended, then add flour, salt and baking soda. Cover and chill dough for 2 to 3 hours. Unwrap all the Snickers. Remove dough from the refrigerator. Divide into 1 tablespoon pieces and flatten. Place a Snickers in the center of each piece of dough. Form the dough into a ball around each Snickers. Place on a greased cookie sheet and bake at 350° for 10 to 12 minutes. Let cookies cool on baking rack or waxed paper.

PERSIMMON COOKIES   *Lilly*

½ c. shortening
1 egg
1 tsp. baking soda
¼ tsp. cloves
½ tsp. salt
1 c. persimmon pulp
1 c. sugar
2 c. flour
½ tsp. cinnamon
¼ tsp. nutmeg
½ c. pecans
½ c. raisins

Cream together shortening, sugar and egg, then add all other ingredients. Drop a teaspoonful of mix 2 inches apart on a greased cookie sheet. Bake 15 minutes at 350°.

GHOST IN THE GRAVEYARD

Rhonda Pierce

3 ½ c. cold milk
1 (16-oz.) pkg. Oreo cookies
1 (12-oz.) tub Cool Whip

2 (4-oz.) pkgs. chocolate instant
pudding

Crunch cookies in a plastic wrap with a rolling pin or in a food processor. Mix pudding with milk. Let stand for 5 minutes. Stir in 3 cups of Cool Whip and ½ of the cookies. Spoon into 13 x 9-inch dish. Sprinkle with remaining cookies. Refrigerate for 1 hour. Decorate with candy (gummy worms) and/or rectangular sandwich cookies (tombstones) and spoonfuls of Cool Whip (ghosts). Serves 12.

OATMEAL COOKIES

Beat thoroughly:

¾ c. shortening
½ c. white sugar
¼ c. water

1 c. brown sugar
1 egg
1 tsp. vanilla

Mix well:

1 c. flour
½ tsp. soda

1 tsp. salt

Mix all ingredients. Blend in 3 cups oats. Bake in 350° oven for 12 to 15 minutes.

NO-BAKE COOKIES

½ c. margarine
½ c. milk

2 c. sugar

Combine in saucepan. Boil 3 to 4 minutes, stirring constantly. Remove from heat.

¾ c. peanut butter
6 T. cocoa

1 tsp. vanilla

Add the above ingredients into the first 3 ingredients. Fold in 3 quick oats. Drop by spoonfuls onto wax paper.

MOLASSES COOKIES
(Spicy & Old Fashioned)

3 ½ c. all-purpose flour
1 ½ tsp. cinnamon
1 c. shortening
⅔ c. brown sugar, firmly packed

1 c. thick buttermilk
2 tsp. soda
½ tsp. salt
1 c. molasses

First grease 1 or 2 baking sheets to have handy. Sift and measure flour; add soda, cinnamon and salt. Sift and set aside. Cream shortening. Blend in sugar gradually, then the molasses and mix well. Mix in about ⅓ of the flour, then ½ of the buttermilk. Repeat. Finish blending in the remaining flour. Drop by rounded tablespoon on baking sheet about ½ inch apart. Spread slightly with back of spoon. Bake in preheated oven at 375° for 12 to 15 minutes, or until lightly brown. Cool thoroughly before storing in covered container.

126207-15

CHINESE COOKIE
Betty Gallagher

3 pkgs. butterscotch chips   **2 T. peanut butter**

Mix together in double boiler. When blended, stir in 1 large can chow mein noodles and drop by spoonful onto wax paper.

CHOCOLATE CHIP PUMPKIN COOKIES

1 pkg. spice cake mix   **1 (15-oz.) can pumpkin**
1 c. chocolate chips or more

Empty contents of cake mix box into bowl, then add the can of pumpkin and thoroughly mix together. Add chocolate chips. Drop by heaping teaspoonful on vegetable oil-sprayed cookie sheet and bake in 350° oven for 20 minutes. Let sit on cookie sheet after removing from oven for a couple of minutes, then cool on a cookie rack. There are no other ingredients as you **do not** use any eggs, oil, liquid or anything listed on the cake mix box, nor do you add anything to the can of pumpkin. They turn out wonderful. Enjoy. **Optional:** You can make a variety of different cookies by using 1¾ to 2 cups of applesauce, persimmon pulp, pinto beans, mashed, apple pie filling (chopped apples) or experiment with different things.

HOMEMADE "SNOW" ICE CREAM
Rhonda Pierce

12-oz. can evaporated milk   **1 c. sugar**
1 bottle vanilla   **Snow**

In a large plastic bowl, mix 1 tablespoon sugar to each heaping cupful of clean fine snow (no yellow snow). Slowly mix evaporated milk into the snow as you stir. Mix in only enough to hold the fine snow together and it will start looking like real ice cream. Add 2 tablespoons of vanilla first, then you can add more to your own taste. It is now ready to eat. Dig in!

PECAN BARK

1 c. unsalted butter   **24 graham cracker squares**
1 c. firmly packed brown sugar   **1 c. chopped pecans**

Preheat oven to 350°. Line a 10 x 15-inch cookie sheet with aluminum foil. Lightly grease foil. Place graham cracker on the cookie sheet in one layer (24 should easily fit). Sprinkle pecans evenly over the top and set aside. Melt butter in a small saucepan. Add brown sugar and stir until mixture boils. Boil 1 minute. Pour mixture evenly over graham crackers and pecans. Bake for 10 minutes. Remove from oven and immediately place hot cookie sheet in the freezer. Remove the pan after 1 hour and break the bark into pieces. This candy doesn't need to be refrigerated.

MOM'S CHOCOLATE GRAVY
Janice Pelham

5 heaping T. cocoa
1 heaping c. granulated sugar

1 c. flour
1 c. water

Mix well. Bring to a boil. Turn to medium heat. Stir gently to keep from sticking until thickened. Serve over hot biscuits with dab of butter.

PRETZEL CANDY

Sm. pretzels or sm. butter cookie
Rolo candy

Pecans or walnuts

Put sheet of foil on cookie sheet. Put a single layer of pretzels or cookies. Unwrap Rolo candy and place on each pretzel or cookie. Heat oven to 350°. Place cookie sheet in oven for 2 to 3 minutes. Remove and place a nut on each candy and smash down. (I place cookie sheet in refrigerator until firm.) Remove candy and enjoy.

TOFFEE
Sharon Broyles

1 c. raw sugar
¼ c. water
2 tsp. vanilla

1 lb. butter
2 tsp. almond extract
Sliced almonds, toasted

Place some sliced almonds on cookie sheet. Put into a 350° oven until toasted, about 10 minutes. Reserve some of the toasted almonds to sprinkle on top of candy at the end. In a medium-size saucepan, put sugar, butter and water. Using a thermometer, cook toffee to the hard crack stage (310°), stirring constantly for about 10 to 20 minutes. Candy will start to bubble hard as it gets hot, so use the appropriate size pan. Be sure to remember almonds in oven. When they get browned, take out of oven. When candy is ready, add in the almond and vanilla extracts. Stir, then take off stove and pour over the toasted almonds on cookie sheet. Melt some chocolate chips in microwave or on top of stove. Spread on top of candy. Sprinkle some of the almonds on top. Let candy harden and crack into small pieces.

SARAH'S SNICKERDOODLES COOKIES
Sarah Ash

1 c. butter
2 eggs
1 tsp. soda
½ tsp. salt
1 ½ c. sugar

2 ¾ c. flour
2 tsp. cream of tartar
2 T. sugar
2 T. cinnamon

Heat oven to 375°. Mix 2 tablespoons sugar with 2 tablespoons cinnamon; set aside. Mix flour, cream of tartar, soda and salt. Set aside. Mix butter and sugar thoroughly. Add eggs and stir well. Add dry ingredients to this mixture, stirring well. Form into balls about the size of a walnut and roll in the sugar and cinnamon mixture. Place about 2 inches apart on an ungreased cookie sheet. Bake 8 to 10 minutes.

126207-15

RAW SPANISH PEANUT BRITTLE

2 c. sugar
2 c. raw peanuts

1 c. white Karo syrup
2 tsp. soda

Cook sugar and water until it spins like a thread. Add peanuts and cook until light brown in color. Remove from heat and fold in butter, soda, vanilla and dash of salt. Quickly pour into buttered cookie sheet. Let it spread itself, allow to harden.

PERSIMMON FRUIT CAKE
Lucy Bowen

2 c. persimmon pulp
2 tsp. soda
3 c. flour
2 tsp. baking powder
2 eggs
2 c. sugar
1 tsp. cinnamon

½ tsp. nutmeg
¼ tsp. salt
2 tsp. vanilla
1 c. cherries, dried
1 c. raisins
1 c. crushed pineapple
1 c. nuts, chopped

Mix soda in persimmon pulp and let stand while mixing other ingredients together. Grease well 2 loaf or 10-inch tube pan. Bake 45 minutes in 350° oven until done.

MAY ROBISON'S EASY NO-BAKE CHEESECAKE

Ready crust, 2 extra servings
2 Philadelphia cream cheese bricks
1 can Eagle Brand sweetened
  condensed milk

½ c. lemon juice
1 (8-oz.) tub Cool Whip
1 can of your favorite pie filling,
  chilled

Cream together the cream cheese and Eagle Brand milk, then add ½ cup lemon juice and mix thoroughly, then stir in Cool Whip. Pour mixture into ready crust and refrigerate for 2 hours. Serve plain or pour chilled pie filling over top. Blueberry cheesecake is my favorite!

JIF PEANUT BUTTER CEREAL BITES
Lilly, Suzzie & Cherrie Moore

¾ c. Jif creamy peanut butter
¼ c. butter, softened
1 ¼ c. Kellogg's Jif peanut butter
  cereal, crushed to 1 c.

1 c. powdered sugar
¾ c. chocolate sprinkles or multi-
  colored sprinkles

In a large mixer bowl, combine peanut butter and butter. Beat on medium speed of electric mixer until well mixed. Add crushed cereal and powdered sugar. Beat until well mixed. Place sprinkles on shallow dish. Shape peanut butter mixture into 1-inch balls. Roll in sprinkles and place on wax paper-lined baking sheet. Refrigerate at least 2 hours. Store in tightly covered container in refrigerator. Makes 30 servings.

HELLO DOLLY
Alice Banning

1 cube margarine or butter
1 c. graham cracker crumbs
1 c. shredded coconut

1 c. chocolate chips
1 c. nuts
1 c. Eagle Brand milk

Layer ingredients in order called for. Cover with evaporated milk. Bake at 375° for 30 minutes. Cool, cut into small squares. Very rich.

PEACH CAKE

3 eggs, well beaten
1 ¾ c. sugar
1 c. cooking oil
2 c. flour
1 tsp. salt

1 tsp. cinnamon
2 c. sliced peaches
½ c. chopped nuts
1 tsp. soda

Mix thoroughly by hand. Pour in greased and floured 13 x 9-inch pan. Bake at 375° for 50 minutes.

PERSIMMON COOKIES
(Diabetic)

2 c. Splenda
1 c. oil
2 c. persimmon pulp or slightly
   more
2 tsp. baking soda, mixed with pulp
2 eggs
4 c. flour

2 tsp. cinnamon
1 tsp. cloves
1 tsp. nutmeg
1 tsp. salt
2 c. chopped pecans or walnuts
2 c. raisins
1 T. vanilla (opt.)

Cream together sugar and oil. Mix persimmon pulp with soda. Add eggs, vanilla and sugar mixture. Mix in pulp. Combine flour, cinnamon, cloves, nutmeg and salt. Combine with egg mixture. Add nuts and raisins. Drop by spoonfuls on greased cookie sheet. Bake at 350° for 12 to 15 minutes.

CRACK
Trisha Yearwood's Recipe
Alice Banning

Layer saltine crackers in bottom of 9 x 13-inch foil pan in single layer close together touching sides. Cook 1 cup brown sugar and 2 cubes of butter. Mix and cook until caramel color and pulls away from sides of pan, just a couple of minutes of boiling. Pour over crackers. Spread. Preheat oven to 425°. Cook 5 minutes on bottom shelf of oven. Remove. Cover with 1 to 1½ cups of chocolate chips. Let start to melt, then spread over caramel. Put in freezer to cool. Frost. Break into pieces, any shape or size.

126207-15

OATMEAL COOKIES

¾ c. shortening
1 c. brown sugar
½ c. white sugar
1 egg
¼ c. water

1 tsp. vanilla
1 c. flour
1 tsp. salt
½ tsp. soda

Beat thoroughly. Mix well. Blend in 3 cups oats. Bake at 350° for 12 to 15 minutes.

PERFECT PIE CRUST   *Edna Welch*

4 c. all-purpose flour, not self-
  rising, do not sift
1 tsp. sugar
½ tsp. salt
1 ¾ c. all vegetable shortening (do
  not use oil or lard or butter)

⅓ c. vinegar
1 lg. egg
½ c. water

Beat together egg and water. Mix all together to crumble stage. Add crust mixture. Mix well. Divide dough into 5 equal parts. Wrap in wax paper or plastic wrap. Refrigerate for 30 minutes. Lightly flour bread board and pat rolls out. Will keep in refrigerator for 3 days. Can be frozen. Makes 5 crusts.

PEANUT BRITTLE   *Edna Welch*

2 c. sugar
1 c. corn syrup
½ c. water

1 c. butter (2 sticks)
2 c. raw peanuts
1 tsp. soda

Heat. Stir sugar, syrup and water in a 3-quart saucepan until dissolved and boils. Blend soft butter. Stir often, until 230°. Add nuts at 280°. Stir constantly to hard crack stage at 305°. Remove from heat. Quickly add soda. Stir for 30 seconds. Pour onto 2 greased cookie sheets.

PECAN BARK

1 c. salted butter
1 c. firmly packed brown sugar

1 c. chopped pecans
26 graham crackers

Preheat oven to 350°. Line a 10 x 15-inch cookie sheet with aluminum foil. Lightly grease foil. Place graham crackers on foil cookie sheet in single layer. Sprinkle pecans evenly over the top and set aside. Melt butter in small pan. Add brown sugar and stir until mixture boils. Boil 1 minute. Pour mixture over graham crackers and pecans. Bake 10 minutes. Remove from oven and put in freezer for 1 hour. Then break apart.

BLACK FOREST CAKE

Lilly

1 box chocolate cake mix　　　　　　**2 (16 oz.) Cool Whip**
2 cans cherries (pie filling kind)

Mix cake according to box. Bake in 9-inch round pans. Let cool. Make a hold in the center of first layer. Fill with cherries. Cover with Cool Whip. Do the same with second layer after you put on top of first. Save the cake crumbles for sides. Cover with Cool Whip. Place crumbles on sides.

126207-15

This & That

Helpful Hints

- Never overcook foods that are to be frozen. Foods will finish cooking when reheated. Don't refreeze cooked, thawed foods.

- When freezing foods, label each container with its contents and the date it was put into the freezer. Always use frozen, cooked foods within 1−2 months.

- To avoid teary eyes when cutting onions, cut them under cold running water or briefly place them in the freezer before cutting.

- Fresh lemon juice will remove onion scent from hands.

- To get the most juice out of fresh lemons, bring them to room temperature and roll them under your palm against the kitchen counter before cutting and squeezing.

- Add raw rice to the salt shaker to keep the salt free flowing.

- Transfer jelly and salad dressings to small plastic squeeze bottles − no more messy, sticky jars!

- Ice cubes will help sharpen garbage disposal blades.

- Separate stuck-together glasses by filling the inside glass with cold water and setting both in hot water.

- Clean CorningWare® by filling it with water and dropping in two denture cleaning tablets. Let stand for 30−45 minutes.

- Always spray your grill with nonstick cooking spray before grilling to avoid sticking.

- To make a simple polish for copper bottom cookware, mix equal parts of flour and salt with vinegar to create a paste.

- Purchase a new coffee grinder and mark it "spices." It can be used to grind most spices; however, cinnamon bark, nutmeg, and others must be broken up a little first. Clean the grinder after each use.

- In a large shaker, combine 6 parts salt and 1 part pepper for quick and easy seasoning.

- Save your store-bought bread bags and ties—they make perfect storage bags for homemade bread.

- Next time you need a quick ice pack, grab a bag of frozen peas or other vegetables out of the freezer.

THIS & THAT

INDIVIDUAL HAM & EGG MUFFINS

36 Tater Tots
½ c. diced peppers
¼ c. milk
Salt to taste

½ c. diced ham
7 eggs
¼ c. shredded cheddar cheese
Pepper to taste

Preheat oven to 400°. Grease a muffin pan liberally. These tend to stick, so you can also use a cupcake liner, but add 5 minutes to 20 minutes cook time. Place 3 frozen Tater Tots in the bottom of each muffin tin and bake for 10 minutes. Remove and press the Tots down to form a base, using a glass or measuring cup. Return to oven and bake for 5 more minutes. Remove from oven. Reduce oven temperature to 350°. Top each cup with about ½ tablespoon of diced ham and ½ tablespoon of diced peppers. Whisk together the eggs and milk and pour the mixture into each muffin tin nearly to the top. Sprinkle each with a little shredded cheese.

1968 AUNT HATTIE HOSMAN'S PANCAKES

Peggy Hosman

1 c. flour
2 tsp. baking powder
2 tsp. oil

2 tsp. sugar
1 egg
Enough milk to your liking (thin fat)

Mix ingredients. Heat oiled pan until drop of water spits. Serve buttered with syrup or powdered sugar, jelly or peanut butter. Serves 2. Makes 4 pancakes.

HASH BROWN & EGG CASSEROLE

Alice Hopfe

1 c. thawed hash browns
½ c. shredded cheese

5 eggs in ½ c. milk, whipped
1 lb. cooked brown sausage

Layer hash browns, cheese and egg mixture in ungreased pie pan. Bake at 350° for 35 to 40 minutes. Enjoy.

SOUFFLÉ

Alice Banning

1 lb. cheddar cheese, grated
3 eggs
1 c. Bisquick

1 c. diced chilies
3 c. milk

Put chilies and cheese in 9 x 13-inch pan. Blend eggs, milk and Bisquick and pour over chilies and cheese. Bake at 350° about 45 minutes.

MAY ROBISON'S LEMONADE

6 ½ c. water
1 c. lemon juice
1 c. sugar

4 scoops Country Time
1 lemon, peeled and cut into sm. pieces

Refrigerate or serve over ice. Makes 2 quarts.

MAY ROBISON'S PARTY PUNCH

1 gal. Hi-C or Hawaiian Punch   ½ gal. sherbet
2 L. 7-Up

Mix punch and 7-Up together, then float sherbet on top. Depending on your color theme: green punch, lime sherbet; orange punch, orange sherbet; pink/red punch, raspberry sherbet; any color punch, rainbow sherbet.

WASSAIL   *Alice Banning*

2 qt. warm water   2 scant c. sugar, dissolved in 12 oz.
Frozen orange juice   water
½ c. lemon juice   2 sticks cinnamon
1 button ginger   10 allspice beans

Boil spices in 1 quart of water, then strain. Add ½ gallon of apple cider to the spiced water. Warm all together. Makes 20 small cups. Keep and use water from spices and toss spices away.

OMELET BREAKFAST BITES

36 Tater Tots   ¼ c. milk
½ c. diced ham   ¼ c. shredded cheddar cheese
½ c. diced peppers   Salt to taste
7 eggs   Pepper to taste

Preheat oven to 400°. Grease a muffin pan liberally. These tend to stick, so you can also use a cupcake liner, but add 5 minutes to 20 minutes cook time. Place 3 frozen Tater Tots in the bottom of each muffin tin and bake for 10 minutes. Remove and press the Tots down to form a base, using a glass or measuring cup. Return to oven and bake 5 more minutes. Remove from oven. Reduce oven temperature to 350°. Top each cup with about ½ tablespoon of diced ham and ½ tablespoon of diced peppers. Whisk together the eggs and milk and pour mixture into each muffin tin nearly to the top. Sprinkle each with a little shredded cheese. Bake for 20 minutes, or until egg is cooked.

NICKELODEON GAK
(Copy Kat Recipes)

1 c. white Elmer's Glue   Food color
1 c. liquid starch (Sta-Flo works the
   best)

Put glue and food coloring in a plastic container. Add starch, a little at a time, stirring constantly. Keep stirring until mixture holds together like putty. Test with fingers. If it is too sticky, add more starch in small amounts until mass is smooth and rubbery. Gak is kind of like "Slime". It is a sticky, gooey clay-like substance.

FOR DELICIOUS PERSONALITY

3 c. kindness and thoughtfulness
1 ½ c. neatness
1 c. poise

1 c. sense of humor
2 c. honesty
2 tsp. tact

Mix honesty, kindness and thoughtfulness until light and fluffy. Then fold in tact, poise and neatness. Mix thoroughly. Add sense of humor and you have a most satisfactory product.

PLAY DOUGH FOR KIDS
Rhonda Pierce

1 c. flour
2 tsp. cream of tartar
½ c. salt

Food coloring
1 tsp. oil
1 c. water

Mix in Teflon pan and cook over low heat until it forms a ball and mixture is not sticky. Mix with food coloring (your judge of how much coloring you want) to get different colors separate mixture into sections or make several batches of the play dough to use. Store in a sealed (prefer 20-ounce) canister. Great for a rainy day project for you and the kids.

POPCORN BALLS
Rhonda Pierce

2 gal. popped corn
1 cube margarine

1 lg. bag white marshmallows

Place popped corn in large bowl or pan. (I use a large dishpan.) In a large pot, place margarine and marshmallows. Over a low to medium heat, melt, stirring constantly, to keep from burning. When melted, pour over the popped corn. Wear rubber or plastic gloves, buttering hands and form into ball. Wrap with Saran Wrap. Food coloring can be added to marshmallow mix: Christmas balls, red or green; Easter balls, pink, blue, yellow or green; Halloween, orange or black; Valentines Day, red; St. Patrick's Day, green.

HOME HAPPINESS CAKE
Lucy Bowen

Take 1 cup of common sense and ½ cup of justice and ½ cup of love. Sift with 1 ½ teaspoons of mutual confidence. Add 2 large portions of sense of humor, beaten separately. Spice to taste with nonsense. Bake in moderate oven of warm approval. Ice with generous appreciation.

RECIPE FOR LIVING

1 full c. of love	1 lb. humility
¼ c. will power	A sprinkling of common sense
3 oz. determination	A pinch of adventure
A dash of flexibility	1 full (8-oz.) can foresight
1 lg. head understanding	A hint of hindsight
A few leaves of awareness (fresh if possible)	A few sprigs of humor, seasoned to taste
½ lb. pride, cut into sm. portions	

Sauté love and understanding until tender. Mix well and continue cooking gently. In a large bowl, blend will power and determination well to avoid procrastination, adding a dash of flexibility to accommodate life's delicate variations. Fold in a few leaves of awareness more if you savor knowledge. Set aside to rise and extend its flavor throughout the days. In a separate bowl, combine pride, whisked lightly with humility. Pour in common sense and sprinkle lightly with adventure. Set oven with foresight for each new day but hindsight just enough to profit from the old. Season entire mixture with humor. Bake for 24 hours, testing often and adjusting to the wonder of each new day.

RECIPE FOR A HOME

½ c. of friendship	Be sure to add a spoonful each
Add a cup of thoughtfulness	Of gaiety that sings
Cream together with a	And also the ability to laugh
Pinch of powdered tenderness	At little things.
Very lightly beaten	Moisten with the sudden tears
In a bowl of loyalty	Of heartfelt sympathy.
With a cup of faith, one of hope	Bake in good-natured pan
And one of charity.	And serve repeatedly.

FRENCH TOAST SANDWICHES   *M. Smith*

8 slices bread	Sausage patties, cooked, enough to cover slice of bread x 4
8 or 10 eggs	
4 slices cheese	

Beat eggs with 1 teaspoon salt. Make 9 slices French toast. Set aside in warm oven. Cook remaining beaten eggs in large skillet or griddle, consistency of thin omelet. Divide egg into fourths. Fold onto open-face French toast. Place cheese and sausage on egg. Put on toast "top". Serve on plates with maple syrup to dip. Serves 4.

PRESERVED CHILDREN

Take 1 large field, half dozen children, 2 or 3 small dogs, a pinch of brook and some pebbles. Mix the children and dogs together; put them on the field, stirring constantly. Pour the brook over the pebbles. Sprinkle the field with flowers. Spread over all a deep blue sky and bake in the sun. When brown, set away to cool in the bath tub.

126207-15

SOUFFLÉ

Alice Banning

1 lb. cheddar cheese, grated
1 c. diced chilies
3 eggs

3 c. milk
1 c. Bisquick

Put chiles and cheese in 9 x 13-inch pan. Blend eggs, milk and Bisquick and pour over chilies and cheese. Bake at 350° about 45 minutes.

Recipe Favorites

126207-15

INDEX OF RECIPES

MAIN DISHES

BREADS & ROLLS

126207-15

THIS & THAT

126207-15

PANTRY BASICS

A WELL-STOCKED PANTRY provides all the makings for a good meal. With the right ingredients, you can quickly create a variety of satisfying, delicious meals for family or guests. Keeping these items in stock also means avoiding extra trips to the grocery store, saving you time and money. Although everyone's pantry is different, there are basic items you should always have. Add other items according to your family's needs. For example, while some families consider chips, cereals and snacks as must-haves, others can't be without feta cheese and imported olives. Use these basic pantry suggestions as a handy reference list when creating your grocery list. Don't forget refrigerated items like milk, eggs, cheese and butter.

STAPLES

Baker's chocolate

Baking powder

Baking soda

Barbeque sauce

Bread crumbs (plain or seasoned)

Chocolate chips

Cocoa powder

Cornmeal

Cornstarch

Crackers

Flour

Honey

Ketchup

Lemon juice

Mayonnaise or salad dressing

Non-stick cooking spray

Nuts (almonds, pecans, walnuts)

Oatmeal

Oil (olive, vegetable)

Pancake baking mix

Pancake syrup

Peanut butter

Shortening

Sugar (granulated, brown, powdered)

Vinegar

PACKAGED/CANNED FOODS

Beans (canned, dry)

Broth (beef, chicken)

Cake mixes with frosting

Canned diced tomatoes

Canned fruit

Canned mushrooms

Canned soup

Canned tomato paste & sauce

Canned tuna & chicken

Cereal

Dried soup mix

Gelatin (flavored or plain)

Gravies

Jarred Salsa

Milk (evaporated, sweetened condensed)

Non-fat dry milk

Pastas

Rice (brown, white)

Spaghetti sauce

SPICES/SEASONINGS

Basil

Bay leaves

Black pepper

Bouillon cubes (beef, chicken)

Chives

Chili powder

Cinnamon

Mustard (dried, prepared)

Garlic powder or salt

Ginger

Nutmeg

Onion powder or salt

Oregano

Paprika

Parsley

Rosemary

Sage

Salt

Soy sauce

Tarragon

Thyme

Vanilla

Worcestershire sauce

Yeast

HERBS & SPICES

DRIED VS. FRESH. While dried herbs are convenient, they don't generally have the same purity of flavor as fresh herbs. Ensure dried herbs are still fresh by checking if they are green and not faded. Crush a few leaves to see if the aroma is still strong. Always store them in an air-tight container away from light and heat.

BASIL
Sweet, warm flavor with an aromatic odor. Use whole or ground. Good with lamb, fish, roast, stews, beef, vegetables, dressing and omelets.

BAY LEAVES
Pungent flavor. Use whole leaf but remove before serving. Good in vegetable dishes, seafood, stews and pickles.

CARAWAY
Spicy taste and aromatic smell. Use in cakes, breads, soups, cheese and sauerkraut.

CELERY SEED
Strong taste which resembles the vegetable. Can be used sparingly in pickles and chutney, meat and fish dishes, salads, bread, marinades, dressings and dips.

CHIVES
Sweet, mild flavor like that of onion. Excellent in salads, fish, soups and potatoes.

CILANTRO
Use fresh. Excellent in salads, fish, chicken, rice, beans and Mexican dishes.

CINNAMON
Sweet, pungent flavor. Widely used in many sweet baked goods, chocolate dishes, cheesecakes, pickles, chutneys and hot drinks.

CORIANDER
Mild, sweet, orangy flavor and available whole or ground. Common in curry powders and pickling spice and also used in chutney, meat dishes, casseroles, Greek-style dishes, apple pies and baked goods.

CURRY POWDER
Spices are combined to proper proportions to give a distinct flavor to meat, poultry, fish and vegetables.

DILL
Both seeds and leaves are flavorful. Leaves may be used as a garnish or cooked with fish, soup, dressings, potatoes and beans. Leaves or the whole plant may be used to flavor pickles.

FENNEL
Sweet, hot flavor. Both seeds and leaves are used. Use in small quantities in pies and baked goods. Leaves can be boiled with fish.

HERBS & SPICES

GINGER — A pungent root, this aromatic spice is sold fresh, dried or ground. Use in pickles, preserves, cakes, cookies, soups and meat dishes.

MARJORAM — May be used both dried or green. Use to flavor fish, poultry, omelets, lamb, stew, stuffing and tomato juice.

MINT — Aromatic with a cool flavor. Excellent in beverages, fish, lamb, cheese, soup, peas, carrots and fruit desserts.

NUTMEG — Whole or ground. Used in chicken and cream soups, cheese dishes, fish cakes, and with chicken and veal. Excellent in custards, milk puddings, pies and cakes.

OREGANO — Strong, aromatic odor. Use whole or ground in tomato juice, fish, eggs, pizza, omelets, chili, stew, gravy, poultry and vegetables.

PAPRIKA — A bright red pepper, this spice is used in meat, vegetables and soups or as a garnish for potatoes, salads or eggs.

PARSLEY — Best when used fresh, but can be used dried as a garnish or as a seasoning. Try in fish, omelets, soup, meat, stuffing and mixed greens.

ROSEMARY — Very aromatic. Can be used fresh or dried. Season fish, stuffing, beef, lamb, poultry, onions, eggs, bread and potatoes. Great in dressings.

SAFFRON — Aromatic, slightly bitter taste. Only a pinch needed to flavor and color dishes such as bouillabaisse, chicken soup, rice, paella, fish sauces, buns and cakes. Very expensive, so where a touch of color is needed, use turmeric instead, but the flavor will not be the same.

SAGE — Use fresh or dried. The flowers are sometimes used in salads. May be used in tomato juice, fish, omelets, beef, poultry, stuffing, cheese spreads and breads.

TARRAGON — Leaves have a pungent, hot taste. Use to flavor sauces, salads, fish, poultry, tomatoes, eggs, green beans, carrots and dressings.

THYME — Sprinkle leaves on fish or poultry before broiling or baking. Throw a few sprigs directly on coals shortly before meat is finished grilling.

TURMERIC — Aromatic, slightly bitter flavor. Should be used sparingly in curry powder and relishes and to color cakes and rice dishes.

Use 3 times more fresh herbs if substituting fresh for dried.

BAKING BREADS

HINTS FOR BAKING BREADS

• Kneading dough for 30 seconds after mixing improves the texture of baking powder biscuits.

• Instead of shortening, use cooking or salad oil in waffles and hot cakes.

• When bread is baking, a small dish of water in the oven will help keep the crust from hardening.

• Dip a spoon in hot water to measure shortening, butter, etc., and the fat will slip out more easily.

• Small amounts of leftover corn may be added to pancake batter for variety.

• To make bread crumbs, use the fine cutter of a food grinder and tie a large paper bag over the spout in order to prevent flying crumbs.

• When you are doing any sort of baking, you get better results if you remember to preheat your cookie sheet, muffin tins or cake pans.

3 RULES FOR USE OF LEAVENING AGENTS

1. In simple flour mixtures, use 2 teaspoons baking powder to leaven 1 cup flour. Reduce this amount $1/2$ teaspoon for each egg used.

2. To 1 teaspoon soda, use 2 $1/4$ teaspoons cream of tartar, 2 cups freshly soured milk or 1 cup molasses.

3. To substitute soda and an acid for baking powder, divide the amount of baking powder by 4. Take that as your measure and add acid according to rule 2.

PROPORTIONS OF BAKING POWDER TO FLOUR

biscuits ....to 1 cup flour use 1 $1/4$ tsp. baking powder
cake with oil ....to 1 cup flour use 1 tsp. baking powder
muffins ....to 1 cup flour use 1 $1/2$ tsp. baking powder
popovers ....to 1 cup flour use 1 $1/4$ tsp. baking powder
waffles ....to 1 cup flour use 1 $1/4$ tsp. baking powder

PROPORTIONS OF LIQUID TO FLOUR

pour batter ....to 1 cup liquid use 1 cup flour
drop batter ....to 1 cup liquid use 2 to 2 $1/2$ cups flour
soft dough ....to 1 cup liquid use 3 to 3 $1/2$ cups flour
stiff dough ....to 1 cup liquid use 4 cups flour

TIME & TEMPERATURE CHART

Breads	Minutes	Temperature
biscuits	12 - 15	400° - 450°
cornbread	25 - 30	400° - 425°
gingerbread	40 - 50	350° - 370°
loaf	50 - 60	350° - 400°
nut bread	50 - 75	350°
popovers	30 - 40	425° - 450°
rolls	20 - 30	400° - 450°

BAKING DESSERTS

PERFECT COOKIES

Cookie dough that must be rolled is much easier to handle after it has been refrigerated for 10 to 30 minutes. This keeps the dough from sticking, even though it may be soft. If not done, the soft dough may require more flour and too much flour makes cookies hard and brittle. Place on a floured board only as much dough as can be easily managed. Flour the rolling pin slightly and roll lightly to desired thickness. Cut shapes close together and add trimmings to dough that needs to be rolled. Place pans or sheets in upper third of oven. Watch cookies carefully while baking in order to avoid burned edges. When sprinkling sugar on cookies, try putting it into a salt shaker in order to save time.

PERFECT PIES

• Pie crust will be better and easier to make if all the ingredients are cool.

• The lower crust should be placed in the pan so that it covers the surface smoothly. Air pockets beneath the surface will push the crust out of shape while baking.

• Folding the top crust over the lower crust before crimping will keep juices in the pie.

• When making custard pie, bake at a high temperature for about 10 minutes to prevent a soggy crust. Then finish baking at a low temperature.

• When making cream pie, sprinkle crust with powdered sugar in order to prevent it from becoming soggy.

PERFECT CAKES

• Fill cake pans two-thirds full and spread batter into corners and sides, leaving a slight hollow in the center.

• Cake is done when it shrinks from the sides of the pan or if it springs back when touched lightly with the finger.

• After removing a cake from the oven, place it on a rack for about 5 minutes. Then, the sides should be loosened and the cake turned out on a rack in order to finish cooling.

• Do not frost cakes until thoroughly cool.

• Icing will remain where you put it if you sprinkle cake with powdered sugar first.

TIME & TEMPERATURE CHART

Dessert	Time	Temperature
butter cake, layer	20 - 40 min.	380° - 400°
butter cake, loaf	40 - 60 min.	360° - 400°
cake, angel	50 - 60 min.	300° - 360°
cake, fruit	3 - 4 hrs.	275° - 325°
cake, sponge	40 - 60 min.	300° - 350°
cookies, molasses	18 - 20 min.	350° - 375°
cookies, thin	10 - 12 min.	380° - 390°
cream puffs	45 - 60 min.	300° - 350°
meringue	40 - 60 min.	250° - 300°
pie crust	20 - 40 min.	400° - 500°

VEGETABLES & FRUITS

COOKING TIME TABLE

Vegetable	Cooking Method	Time
artichokes	boiled	40 min.
	steamed	45 - 60 min.
asparagus tips	boiled	10 - 15 min.
beans, lima	boiled	20 - 40 min.
	steamed	60 min.
beans, string	boiled	15 - 35 min.
	steamed	60 min.
beets, old	boiled or steamed	1 - 2 hours.
beets, young with skin	boiled	30 min.
	steamed	60 min.
	baked	70 - 90 min.
broccoli, flowerets	boiled	5 - 10 min.
broccoli, stems	boiled	20 - 30 min.
brussels sprouts	boiled	20 - 30 min.
cabbage, chopped	boiled	10 - 20 min.
	steamed	25 min.
carrots, cut across	boiled	8 - 10 min.
	steamed	40 min.
cauliflower, flowerets	boiled	8 - 10 min.
cauliflower, stem down	boiled	20 - 30 min.
corn, green, tender	boiled	5 - 10 min.
	steamed	15 min.
	baked	20 min.
corn on the cob	boiled	8 - 10 min.
	steamed	15 min.
eggplant, whole	boiled	30 min.
	steamed	40 min.
	baked	45 min.
parsnips	boiled	25 - 40 min.
	steamed	60 min.
	baked	60 - 75 min.
peas, green	boiled or steamed	5 - 15 min.
potatoes	boiled	20 - 40 min.
	steamed	60 min.
	baked	45 - 60 min.
pumpkin or squash	boiled	20 - 40 min.
	steamed	45 min.
	baked	60 min.
tomatoes	boiled	5 - 15 min.
turnips	boiled	25 - 40 min.

DRYING TIME TABLE

Fruit	Sugar or Honey	Cooking Time
apricots	¼ c. for each cup of fruit	about 40 min.
figs	1 T. for each cup of fruit	about 30 min.
peaches	¼ c. for each cup of fruit	about 45 min.
prunes	2 T. for each cup of fruit	about 45 min.

VEGETABLES *&* FRUITS

BUYING FRESH VEGETABLES

Artichokes: Look for compact, tightly closed heads with green, clean-looking leaves. Avoid those with leaves that are brown or separated.

Asparagus: Stalks should be tender and firm; tips should be close and compact. Choose the stalks with very little white; they are more tender. Use asparagus soon because it toughens quickly.

Beans, Snap: Those with small seeds inside the pods are best. Avoid beans with dry-looking pods.

Broccoli, Brussels Sprouts and Cauliflower: Flower clusters on broccoli and cauliflower should be tight and close together. Brussels sprouts should be firm and compact. Smudgy, dirty spots may indicate pests or disease.

Cabbage and Head Lettuce: Choose heads that are heavy for their size. Avoid cabbage with worm holes and lettuce with discoloration or soft rot.

Cucumbers: Choose long, slender cucumbers for best quality. May be dark or medium green, but yellow ones are undesirable

Mushrooms: Caps should be closed around the stems. Avoid black or brown gills.

Peas and Lima Beans: Select pods that are well-filled but not bulging. Avoid dried, spotted, yellow or limp pods.

BUYING FRESH FRUITS

Bananas: Skin should be free of bruises and black or brown spots. Purchase them slightly green and allow them to ripen at room temperature.

Berries: Select plump, solid berries with good color. Avoid stained containers which indicate wet or leaky berries. Berries with clinging caps, such as blackberries and raspberries, may be unripe. Strawberries without caps may be overripe.

Melons: In cantaloupes, thick, close netting on the rind indicates best quality. Cantaloupes are ripe when the stem scar is smooth and the space between the netting is yellow or yellow-green. They are best when fully ripe with fruity odor.

Honeydews are ripe when rind has creamy to yellowish color and velvety texture. Immature honeydews are whitish-green.

Ripe watermelons have some yellow color on one side. If melons are white or pale green on one side, they are not ripe.

Oranges, Grapefruit and Lemons: Choose those heavy for their size. Smoother, thinner skins usually indicate more juice. Most skin markings do not affect quality. Oranges with a slight greenish tinge may be just as ripe as fully colored ones. Light or greenish-yellow lemons are more tart than deep yellow ones. Avoid citrus fruits showing withered, sunken or soft areas.

NAPKIN FOLDING

FOR BEST RESULTS, use well-starched linen napkins if possible. For more complicated folds, 24-inch napkins work best. Practice the folds with newspapers. Children will have fun decorating the table once they learn these attractive folds!

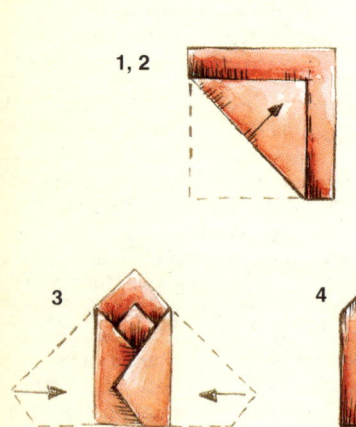

SHIELD

Easy fold. Elegant with monogram in corner.

Instructions:
1. Fold into quarter size. If monogrammed, ornate corner should face down.
2. Turn up folded corner three-quarters.
3. Overlap right side and left side points.
4. Turn over; adjust sides so they are even, single point in center.
5. Place point up or down on plate, or left of plate.

ROSETTE

Elegant on plate.

Instructions:
1. Fold left and right edges to center, leaving 1/2" opening along center.
2. Pleat firmly from top edge to bottom edge. Sharpen edges with hot iron.
3. Pinch center together. If necessary, use small piece of pipe cleaner to secure and top with single flower.
4. Spread out rosette.

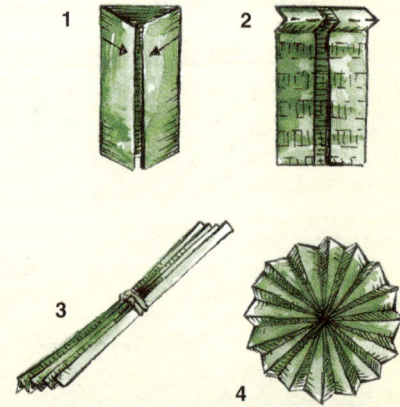

NAPKIN FOLDING

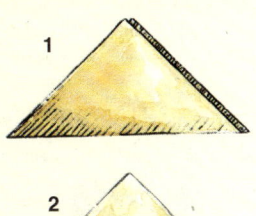

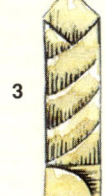

CANDLE

Easy to do; can be decorated.

Instructions:
1. Fold into triangle, point at top.
2. Turn lower edge up 1".
3. Turn over, folded edge down.
4. Roll tightly from left to right.
5. Tuck in corner. Stand upright.

FAN

Pretty in napkin ring or on plate.

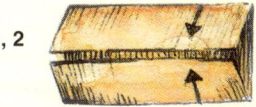

Instructions:
1. Fold top and bottom edges to center.
2. Fold top and bottom edges to center a second time.
3. Pleat firmly from the left edge. Sharpen edges with hot iron.
4. Spread out fan. Balance flat folds of each side on table. Well-starched napkins will hold shape.

LILY

Effective and pretty on table.

Instructions:
1. Fold napkin into quarters.
2. Fold into triangle, closed corner to open points.
3. Turn two points over to other side. (Two points are on either side of closed point.)
4. Pleat.
5. Place closed end in glass. Pull down two points on each side and shape.

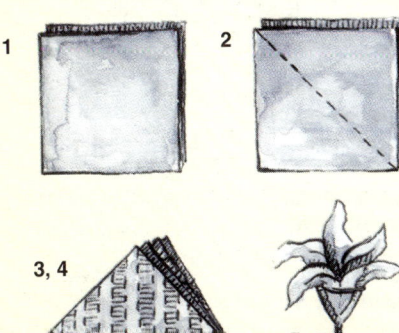

MEASUREMENTS & SUBSTITUTIONS

MEASUREMENTS

a pinch	1/8 teaspoon or less
3 teaspoons	1 tablespoon
4 tablespoons	1/4 cup
8 tablespoons	1/2 cup
12 tablespoons	3/4 cup
16 tablespoons	1 cup
2 cups	1 pint
4 cups	1 quart
4 quarts	1 gallon
8 quarts	1 peck
4 pecks	1 bushel
16 ounces	1 pound
32 ounces	1 quart
1 ounce liquid	2 tablespoons
8 ounces liquid	1 cup

Use standard measuring spoons and cups. All measurements are level.

C° TO F° CONVERSION

120° C	250° F
140° C	275° F
150° C	300° F
160° C	325° F
180° C	350° F
190° C	375° F
200° C	400° F
220° C	425° F
230° C	450° F

Temperature conversions are estimates.

SUBSTITUTIONS

Ingredient	Quantity	Substitute
baking powder	1 teaspoon	1/4 tsp. baking soda plus 1/2 tsp. cream of tartar
chocolate	1 square (1 oz.)	3 or 4 T. cocoa plus 1 T. butter
cornstarch	1 tablespoon	2 T. flour or 2 tsp. quick-cooking tapioca
cracker crumbs	3/4 cup	1 c. bread crumbs
dates	1 lb.	1 1/2 c. dates, pitted and cut
dry mustard	1 teaspoon	1 T. prepared mustard
flour, self-rising	1 cup	1 c. all-purpose flour, 1/2 tsp. salt, and 1 tsp. baking powder
herbs, fresh	1 tablespoon	1 tsp. dried herbs
ketchup or chili sauce	1 cup	1 c. tomato sauce plus 1/2 c. sugar and 2 T. vinegar (for use in cooking)
milk, sour	1 cup	1 T. lemon juice or vinegar plus sweet milk to make 1 c. (let stand 5 minutes)
whole	1 cup	1/2 c. evaporated milk plus 1/2 c. water
min. marshmallows	10	1 lg. marshmallow
onion, fresh	1 small	1 T. instant minced onion, rehydrated
sugar, brown	1/2 cup	2 T. molasses in 1/2 c. granulated sugar
powdered	1 cup	1 c. granulated sugar plus 1 tsp. cornstarch
tomato juice	1 cup	1/2 c. tomato sauce plus 1/2 c. water

When substituting cocoa for chocolate in cakes, the amount of flour must be reduced. Brown and white sugars usually can be interchanged.

EQUIVALENCY CHART

Food	Quantity	Yield
apple	1 medium	1 cup
banana, mashed	1 medium	1/3 cup
bread	1 1/2 slices	1 cup soft crumbs
bread	1 slice	1/4 cup fine, dry crumbs
butter	1 stick or 1/4 pound	1/2 cup
cheese, American, cubed	1 pound	2 2/3 cups
American, grated	1 pound	5 cups
cream cheese	3-ounce package	6 2/3 tablespoons
chocolate, bitter	1 square	1 ounce
cocoa	1 pound	4 cups
coconut	1 1/2 pound package	2 2/3 cups
coffee, ground	1 pound	5 cups
cornmeal	1 pound	3 cups
cornstarch	1 pound	3 cups
crackers, graham	14 squares	1 cup fine crumbs
saltine	28 crackers	1 cup fine crumbs
egg	4-5 whole	1 cup
whites	8-10	1 cup
yolks	10-12	1 cup
evaporated milk	1 cup	3 cups whipped
flour, cake, sifted	1 pound	4 1/2 cups
rye	1 pound	5 cups
white, sifted	1 pound	4 cups
white, unsifted	1 pound	3 3/4 cups
gelatin, flavored	3 1/4 ounces	1/2 cup
unflavored	1/4 ounce	1 tablespoon
lemon	1 medium	3 tablespoon juice
marshmallows	16	1/4 pound
noodles, cooked	8-ounce package	7 cups
uncooked	4 ounces (1 1/2 cups)	2-3 cups cooked
macaroni, cooked	8-ounce package	6 cups
macaroni, uncooked	4 ounces (1 1/4 cups)	2 1/4 cups cooked
spaghetti, uncooked	7 ounces	4 cups cooked
nuts, chopped	1/4 pound	1 cup
almonds	1 pound	3 1/2 cups
walnuts, broken	1 pound	3 cups
walnuts, unshelled	1 pound	1 1/2 to 1 3/4 cups
onion	1 medium	1/2 cup
orange	3-4 medium	1 cup juice
raisins	1 pound	3 1/2 cups
rice, brown	1 cup	4 cups cooked
converted	1 cup	3 1/2 cups cooked
regular	1 cup	3 cups cooked
wild	1 cup	4 cups cooked
sugar, brown	1 pound	2 1/2 cups
powdered	1 pound	3 1/2 cups
white	1 pound	2 cups
vanilla wafers	22	1 cup fine crumbs
zwieback, crumbled	4	1 cup

FOOD QUANTITIES

FOR LARGE SERVINGS

	25 Servings	50 Servings	100 Servings
Beverages:			
coffee	1/2 pound & 1 1/2 gallons water	1 pound & 3 gallons water	2 pounds & 6 gallons water
lemonade	10 - 15 lemons & 1 1/2 gallons water	20 - 30 lemons & 3 gallons water	40 - 60 lemons & 6 gallons water
tea	1/12 pound & 1 1/2 gallons water	1/6 pound & 3 gallons water	1/3 pound & 6 gallons water
Desserts:			
layered cake	1 12" cake	3 10" cakes	6 10" cakes
sheet cake	1 10" x 12" cake	1 12" x 20" cake	2 12" x 20" cakes
watermelon	37 1/2 pounds	75 pounds	150 pounds
whipping cream	3/4 pint	1 1/2 to 2 pints	3 - 4 pints
Ice cream:			
brick	3 1/4 quarts	6 1/2 quarts	13 quarts
bulk	2 1/4 quarts	4 1/2 quarts or 1 1/4 gallons	9 quarts or 2 1/2 gallons
Meat, poultry or fish:			
fish	13 pounds	25 pounds	50 pounds
fish, fillets or steak	7 1/2 pounds	15 pounds	30 pounds
hamburger	9 pounds	18 pounds	35 pounds
turkey or chicken	13 pounds	25 - 35 pounds	50 - 75 pounds
wieners (beef)	6 1/2 pounds	13 pounds	25 pounds
Salads, casseroles:			
baked beans	3/4 gallon	1 1/4 gallons	2 1/2 gallons
jello salad	3/4 gallon	1 1/4 gallons	2 1/2 gallons
potato salad	4 1/4 quarts	2 1/4 gallons	4 1/2 gallons
scalloped potatoes	4 1/2 quarts or 1 12" x 20" pan	9 quarts or 2 1/4 gallons	18 quarts 4 1/2 gallons
spaghetti	1 1/4 gallons	2 1/2 gallons	5 gallons
Sandwiches:			
bread	50 slices or 3 1-lb. loaves	100 slices or 6 1-lb. loaves	200 slices or 12 1-lb. loaves
butter	1/2 pound	1 pound	2 pounds
lettuce	1 1/2 heads	3 heads	6 heads
mayonnaise	1 cup	2 cups	4 cups
mixed filling			
meat, eggs, fish	1 1/2 quarts	3 quarts	6 quarts
jam, jelly	1 quart	2 quarts	4 quarts

QUICK FIXES

PRACTICALLY EVERYONE has experienced that dreadful moment in the kitchen when a recipe failed and dinner guests have arrived. Perhaps a failed timer, distraction or a missing or mismeasured ingredient is to blame. These handy tips can save the day!

Acidic foods – Sometimes a tomato-based sauce will become too acidic. Add baking soda, one teaspoon at a time, to the sauce. Use sugar as a sweeter alternative.

Burnt food on pots and pans – Allow the pan to cool on its own. Remove as much of the food as possible. Fill with hot water and add a capful of liquid fabric softener to the pot; let it stand for a few hours. You'll have an easier time removing the burnt food.

Chocolate seizes – Chocolate can seize (turn coarse and grainy) when it comes into contact with water. Place seized chocolate in a metal bowl over a large saucepan with an inch of simmering water in it. Over medium heat, slowly whisk in warm heavy cream. Use 1/4 cup cream to 4 ounces of chocolate. The chocolate will melt and become smooth.

Forgot to thaw whipped topping – Thaw in microwave for 1 minute on the defrost setting. Stir to blend well. Do not over thaw!

Hands smell like garlic or onion – Rinse hands under cold water while rubbing them with a large stainless steel spoon.

Hard brown sugar – Place in a paper bag and microwave for a few seconds, or place hard chunks in a food processor.

Jell-O too hard – Heat on a low microwave power setting for a very short time.

Lumpy gravy or sauce – Use a blender, food processor or simply strain.

No tomato juice – Mix 1/2 cup ketchup with 1/2 cup water.

Out of honey – Substitute 1 1/4 cups sugar dissolved in 1 cup water.

Overcooked sweet potatoes or carrots – Softened sweet potatoes and carrots make a wonderful soufflé with the addition of eggs and sugar. Consult your favorite cookbook for a good soufflé recipe. Overcooked sweet potatoes can also be used as pie filling.

Sandwich bread is stale – Toast or microwave bread briefly. Otherwise, turn it into bread crumbs. Bread exposed to light and heat will hasten its demise, so consider using a bread box. If the bread will not be eaten within a few days, store half in the freezer.

Soup, sauce, gravy too thin – Add 1 tablespoon of flour to hot soup, sauce or gravy. Whisk well (to avoid lumps) while the mixture is boiling. Repeat if necessary.

Sticky rice – Rinse rice with warm water.

Stew or soup is greasy – Refrigerate and remove grease once it congeals. Another trick is to lay cold lettuce leaves over the hot stew for about 10 seconds and then remove. Repeat as necessary.

Too salty – Add a little sugar and vinegar. For soups or sauces, add a raw peeled potato.

Too sweet – Add a little vinegar or lemon juice.

Undercooked cakes and cookies – Serve over vanilla ice cream. You can also layer pieces of cake or cookies with whipped cream and fresh fruit to form a dessert parfait. Crumbled cookies also make an excellent ice cream or cream pie topping.

COUNTING CALORIES

BEVERAGES

apple juice, 6 oz. 90
coffee (black) 0
cola, 12 oz. 115
cranberry juice, 6 oz. 115
ginger ale, 12 oz. 115
grape juice, (prepared from
    frozen concentrate), 6 oz. 142
lemonade, (prepared from
    frozen concentrate), 6 oz. 85
milk, protein fortified, 1 c. 105
    skim, 1 c. 90
    whole, 1 c. 160
orange juice, 6 oz. 85
pineapple juice, unsweetened, 6 oz. 95
root beer, 12 oz. 150
tonic (quinine water) 12 oz. 132

BREADS

cornbread, 1 sm. square 130
dumplings, 1 med. 70
French toast, 1 slice 135
melba toast, 1 slice 25
muffins, blueberry, 1 muffin 110
    bran, 1 muffin.................................106
    corn, 1 muffin.................................125
    English, 1 muffin 280
pancakes, 1 (4-in.) 60
pumpernickel, 1 slice 75
rye, 1 slice 60
waffle, 1 216
white, 1 slice ....60 - 70
whole wheat, 1 slice ....55 - 65

CEREALS

cornflakes, 1 c. 105
cream of wheat, 1 c. 120
oatmeal, 1 c. 148
rice flakes, 1 c. 105
shredded wheat, 1 biscuit 100
sugar krisps, 3/4 c. 110

CRACKERS

graham, 1 cracker ....15 - 30
rye crisp, 1 cracker...............................35
saltine, 1 cracker ....17 - 20
wheat thins, 1 cracker 9

DAIRY PRODUCTS

butter or margarine, 1 T. 100
cheese, American, 1 oz. 100
    camembert, 1 oz.............................85
    cheddar, 1 oz. 115
    cottage cheese, 1 oz. 30
    mozzarella, 1 oz. 90
    parmesan, 1 oz. 130
    ricotta, 1 oz. 50
    roquefort, 1 oz. 105
    Swiss, 1 oz. 105
cream, light, 1 T. 30
    heavy, 1 T. 55
    sour, 1 T. 45
hot chocolate, with milk, 1 c. 277
milk chocolate, 1 oz. ....145 - 155
yogurt
    made w/ whole milk, 1 c. ......150 - 165
    made w/ skimmed milk, 1 c. 125

EGGS

fried, 1 lg. 100
poached or boiled, 1 lg. ....75 - 80
scrambled or in omelet, 1 lg. ....110 - 130

FISH & SEAFOOD

bass, 4 oz. 105
salmon, broiled or baked, 3 oz. 155
sardines, canned in oil, 3 oz. 170
trout, fried, 3 1/2 oz. 220
tuna, in oil, 3 oz. 170
    in water, 3 oz. 110

COUNTING CALORIES

FRUITS

apple, 1 med. ....80 - 100
applesauce, sweetened, 1/2 c. ....90 - 115
    unsweetened, 1/2 c. 50
banana, 1 med. 85
blueberries, 1/2 c. 45
cantaloupe, 1/2 c. 24
cherries (pitted), raw, 1/2 c. 40
grapefruit, 1/2 med. 55
grapes, 1/2 c. ....35 - 55
honeydew, 1/2 c. 55
mango, 1 med. 90
orange, 1 med. ....65 - 75
peach, 1 med. 35
pear, 1 med. ....60 - 100
pineapple, fresh, 1/2 c. 40
    canned in syrup, 1/2 c. 95
plum, 1 med. 30
strawberries, fresh, 1/2 c. 30
    frozen and sweetened, 1/2 c. ..120 - 140
tangerine, 1 lg. 39
watermelon, 1/2 c. 42

MEAT & POULTRY

beef, ground (lean), 3 oz. 185
    roast, 3 oz. 185
chicken, broiled, 3 oz. 115
lamb chop (lean), 3 oz. ....175 - 200
steak, sirloin, 3 oz. 175
    tenderloin, 3 oz. 174
    top round, 3 oz. 162
turkey, dark meat, 3 oz. 175
    white meat, 3 oz. 150
veal, cutlet, 3 oz. 156
    roast, 3 oz. 76

NUTS

almonds, 2 T. 105
cashews, 2 T. 100
peanuts, 2 T. 105
peanut butter, 1 T. 95
pecans, 2 T. 95
pistachios, 2 T. 92
walnuts, 2 T. 80

PASTA

macaroni or spaghetti,
    cooked, 3/4 c. 115

SALAD DRESSINGS

blue cheese, 1 T. 70
French, 1 T. 65
Italian, 1 T. 80
mayonnaise, 1 T. 100
olive oil, 1 T. 124
Russian, 1 T. 70
salad oil, 1 T. 120

SOUPS

bean, 1 c. ....130 - 180
beef noodle, 1 c. 70
bouillon and consomme, 1 c. 30
chicken noodle, 1 c. 65
chicken with rice, 1 c. 50
minestrone, 1 c. ....80 - 150
split pea, 1 c. ....145 - 170
tomato with milk, 1 c. 170
vegetable, 1 c. ....80 - 100

VEGETABLES

asparagus, 1 c. 35
broccoli, cooked, 1/2 c. 25
cabbage, cooked, 1/2 c. ....15 - 20
carrots, cooked, 1/2 c. ....25 - 30
cauliflower, 1/2 c. ....10 - 15
corn (kernels), 1/2 c. 70
green beans, 1 c. 30
lettuce, shredded, 1/2 c. 5
mushrooms, canned, 1/2 c. 20
onions, cooked, 1/2 c. 30
peas, cooked, 1/2 c. 60
potato, baked, 1 med. 90
    chips, 8-10 100
    mashed, w/milk & butter, 1 c. ..200 - 300
spinach, 1 c. 40
tomato, raw, 1 med. 25
    cooked, 1/2 c. 30

COOKING TERMS

Au gratin: Topped with crumbs and/or cheese and browned in oven or under broiler.

Au jus: Served in its own juices.

Baste: To moisten foods during cooking with pan drippings or special sauce in order to add flavor and prevent drying.

Bisque: A thick cream soup.

Blanch: To immerse in rapidly boiling water and allow to cook slightly.

Cream: To soften a fat, especially butter, by beating it at room temperature. Butter and sugar are often creamed together, making a smooth, soft paste.

Crimp: To seal the edges of a two-crust pie either by pinching them at intervals with the fingers or by pressing them together with the tines of a fork.

Crudités: An assortment of raw vegetables (i.e. carrots, broccoli, celery, mushrooms) that is served as an hors d'oeuvre, often accompanied by a dip.

Degrease: To remove fat from the surface of stews, soups or stock. Usually cooled in the refrigerator so that fat hardens and is easily removed.

Dredge: To coat lightly with flour, corn-meal, etc.

Entrée: The main course.

Fold: To incorporate a delicate substance, such as whipped cream or beaten egg whites, into another substance without releasing air bubbles. A spatula is used to gently bring part of the mixture from the bottom of the bowl to the top. The process is repeated, while slowly rotating the bowl, until the ingredients are thoroughly blended.

Glaze: To cover with a glossy coating, such as a melted and somewhat diluted jelly for fruit desserts.

Julienne: To cut or slice vegetables, fruits or cheeses into match-shaped slivers.

Marinate: To allow food to stand in a liquid in order to tenderize or to add flavor.

Meuniére: Dredged with flour and sautéed in butter.

Mince: To chop food into very small pieces.

Parboil: To boil until partially cooked; to blanch. Usually final cooking in a seasoned sauce follows this procedure.

Pare: To remove the outermost skin of a fruit or vegetable.

Poach: To cook gently in hot liquid kept just below the boiling point.

Purée: To mash foods by hand by rubbing through a sieve or food mill, or by whirling in a blender or food processor until perfectly smooth.

Refresh: To run cold water over food that has been parboiled in order to stop the cooking process quickly.

Sauté: To cook and/or brown food in a small quantity of hot shortening.

Scald: To heat to just below the boiling point, when tiny bubbles appear at the edge of the saucepan.

Simmer: To cook in liquid just below the boiling point. The surface of the liquid should be barely moving, broken from time to time by slowly rising bubbles.

Steep: To let food stand in hot liquid in order to extract or to enhance flavor, like tea in hot water or poached fruit in syrup.

Toss: To combine ingredients with a repeated lifting motion.

Whip: To beat rapidly in order to incorporate air and produce expansion, as in heavy cream or egg whites.

MICROWAVE HINTS

- Soften hard ice cream by microwaving at 30% power. One pint will take 15–30 seconds; one quart takes 30–45 seconds; one-half gallon takes 45–60 seconds.

- One stick of butter or margarine will soften in 40 seconds when microwaved at 50% power.

- Soften one unwrapped 8-ounce package of cream cheese by placing in a glass bowl and microwaving on high for 15 seconds.

- A carton of whipped topping will thaw in 1 minute on the defrost setting. Whipped topping should be slightly firm in the center, but will blend when stirred. Do not over thaw!

- To scald milk, cook 1 cup for 2–2 1/2 minutes, stirring once each minute.

- Melt half of a 7-ounce jar of marshmallow creme by microwaving on high for 35–40 seconds.

- If Jell-O® has set up too hard, heat on low power for a very short time.

- To soften hardened brown sugar, place package in the microwave and heat for 30 seconds; fluff with a fork and use immediately.

- Warm pancake syrup by heating on high in serving container for 30–60 seconds.

- To restore crystallized honey, heat in a glass jar covered with plastic wrap on high for 30–45 seconds. Repeat if necessary.

- To toast coconut, spread 1/2 cup coconut on a plate and cook for 3–4 minutes, stirring every 30 seconds after 2 minutes. Keep a close watch because it quickly browns.

- To melt chocolate, place 1/2 pound in a glass bowl or measuring cup. Melt uncovered at 50% power for 1–2 minutes; remove and stir. Repeat in 30 second intervals, as needed.

- Plump dried fruits by microwaving 1 cup of water for 1–2 minutes or until boiling. Add 1/2 cup dried fruit and let stand for 5–10 minutes.

- To get more juice out of lemons, microwave on high for 10–20 seconds. Roll on the counter, slice, and juice.

- Crisp stale potato chips, crackers, cookies, or cereal by placing on paper towels and heating in the microwave for 20–30 seconds.

- To make dry bread crumbs, cut 6 slices of bread into 1/2 inch cubes. Microwave in 3-quart casserole for 6–7 minutes or until dry, stirring after 3 minutes. Crush in blender.

- To clean your microwave, heat a glass bowl of water with a small amount of vinegar for 5 minutes. Keep the door closed for 5 more minutes to give the steam time to work. Remove the bowl and use a moist, soapy dish cloth to wipe the inside walls and door of your microwave. Dried food should wipe off easily.

MORRIS PRESS COOKBOOKS

Publish Your Own
COOKBOOK

Churches, schools, organizations, families, and businesses can preserve their favorite recipes by publishing a custom cookbook. Cookbooks make a great **fundraiser** because they are easy to sell and highly profitable. Our low prices also make cookbooks a perfect, affordable **keepsake**. We offer:

- Low prices, high quality, and prompt service.
- Many options and styles to suit your needs.
- An online cookbook builder or we can assist.
- 90 days to pay and a written No-Risk Guarantee.

Request a FREE Cookbook Kit to start

Visit **www.morriscookbooks.com/CB**
or call **800-445-6621, ext. CB**.

All the Ingredients
for Success!®